Unapologetically Me

Unapologetically Me

8 Empowering stories

8 empowered women

Living life on their terms

Compiled by Jennifer Sharp

Inspirational Stories from women who are living life
on their own terms.

Unapologetically Me

Co-authored by

Lori Gatsi-Barnett
Karen Hendriks
Robin Ross
Cheralyn Darcey
Kerrie Atherton
Michelle Worthington
Nana Mulundiki
Amanda Maynard-Schubert

Disclaimer:

This book is intended for adult readers only. It contains descriptions of mental health, drug use, alcoholism, sexual assault, racism.

Some readers may find this distressing. Reader discretion is advised.

This book is sold with the understanding that the authors are not offering any specific personal advice to the reader. For professional advice, seek the service of a suitable, qualified professional practitioner. The authors and publisher disclaim any responsibility for liability, loss or risk, personal or otherwise, that happens as a consequence of the use and application of any contents of this book.

Unapologetically Me

Cover Art © 2022 Carolyn De Ridder
Edited by Kez Wickham St George and Jennifer Sharp

ISBN SC: 978-0-6489045-6-4
ISBN EB: 978-0-6454232-0-4

NATIONAL
LIBRARY
OF AUSTRALIA

A catalogue record for this book
is available from the
National Library of Australia

It's time to stop playing small
and remember that you are the stars,
the moon, and the whole
damn universe.

-spirit daughter

Never apologize for **BEING** who you are

Celebrate **YOU**

100% Unapologetically

Contents

Introduction

It's 2022, and we are continually seeing the powerful feminine energy rising across the globe. We are awakening our dormant hearts and minds that have, for centuries, been suppressed. For too long we have believed that we, as women, are too much, too different, too difficult, too ugly. Believing that who we truly are is wrong.

We are no longer dimming our inner light; we are stepping up and into our own power, regardless of where we are on our journey. We no longer accept being limited to our situations, or the *stations* we once thought were our future lives. Glass ceilings are being broken, societal rules and expectations of who and what a woman should be are being broken down.

No longer are we being quiet, playing the *Good Girl* role once given. We are evolving strongly, individually and as a collective; a movement of women who are willing to do what it takes to follow their souls' calling and stand up proudly to create change on every level – mind, body, and spirit – within themselves and within community. Everyday women, just like you and me. We are all rising.

We no longer play it safe. We no longer stay quiet, or small. As a collective, women now have the resources to move out of a state of survival. We have the resources to invest in ourselves – to heal and to grow. To evolve internally.

When we allow ourselves to simply be us, something sparks within us – it awakens us, igniting our souls. Another ceiling is being cracked, and by sharing our personal story, by sharing our thoughts, experiences, and self-expression, we unconsciously provide a light for others to do so. As a collective of story tellers, souls are being awakened – dreams, desires wonders, and purpose are coming to life like never before.

Together, we heal, grow, evolve, rise, and reclaim who we are. No more living amongst the shadows. Together, we take back our self-belief, our self-worth. We nurture as we gather strength through knowledge, which enables us to lead through empowerment and heart.

Stepping into this space means you become strong enough to be you. To do you. Our reactions to situations come from judgement, trigger responses, a long-held belief system, that we have within ourselves. If we stay in a space of powerlessness, we rely on others to save us, but when we listen to our own inner wisdom and take necessary action, we find we have the knowledge, abilities, and power to change our circumstances.

By giving yourself permission to stand in your truth, you find the answers you seek for your own dreams and aspirations. You let go of unrealistic beliefs of yourself and those around you. You feel pride toward others' accomplishments, and you find ways to support them with their own self-transformation.

As a collective, we have discovered that our way to being *us* is through accepting who we are – through kindness, compassion, and self-love.

The women you will meet within this book are just like you and me – rising to the call. Each woman is embracing who she is, who she has become, totally unapologetically. Each woman is letting go of limiting beliefs, years of societal conditioning, and allowing her heart and internal knowing to lead the way.

Each woman has overcome insurmountable obstacles and challenges, but it is in the evolution of rising above that determines who she is today.

It is my hope that you will find, as a reader, a part of yourself within their words, and this, in turn, will embody within you all you need to show up for yourself each day. To become fully aligned with who you are. You have the knowledge, understanding and knowing to choose what is right for you, what your next step is and how to take it, and how to spend your time and energy that is meaningful to you.

Stand in your truth and break out of your comfort zone. With this comes growth, and you will discover parts of you that have been locked away. By embracing these parts, you will also discover they are your gifts, not your weaknesses. You just needed to find the key to unlock them and enable yourself to come home to *you*. You will reignite your inner light and power. which was always there – it was just hiding in the shadows for a while.

By turning the key and allowing your inner light through, you are leading the way in showing others how to do the same. You are here to lead the way in whatever capacity you can.

Committing to this path of being 100% unapologetically you, by embracing every inch of yourself, inside and out, is far from easy, but it is worth it. It will allow you to listen to, and answer, your soul's calling; to come into alignment, to step into your divine power unconditionally.

It's liberating and is a choice that you consciously make. It will take investing more time, energy, and looking deep within yourself each day. Step after step, you are building *you*.

It is at this deepest level that you give yourself permission, and acceptance, and embrace your knowing that will allow you to live your dreams and shine each step of the way.

Embrace your gifts, your voice – share them with the world. Seek soulful truths and simply be you. You don't have to do this alone. Like the women presented, you won't have to travel this road on your own.

If you are willing to find and embrace a network of others who can support and guide and encourage you along the way, the transition into fully becoming you will be done so much more easily. It will be far from perfect; good days and the not-so-good abound, but with your found tribe, navigation along unknown territory will only serve you to shine more.

Everyone has a story to tell, no matter who you are in life. We each have celebrated success and learned many lessons; no one story is more important than another, yet each can make a difference. Our stories are made up from our own experiences; in the past and in the now – our futures yet to be written. Are you ready to share yours?

As a collection of emotions and experiences that have been written in rawness and authenticity, we are connected – our minds even more enriched than before. By sharing our stories, our challenges and successes, our fears become hopes, our dreams, our power, our awakening into Being. We are all on our own journeys in life, yet, together, we have experienced so many obstacles that could have undone us. Together we rise – we embrace our strengths, our determination, our resilience, achievements, and blessings.

Each woman's story presented here is told with rawness, and comes directly from the heart, regardless of the darkness that may prevail. Each woman has experienced deep lasting trauma, but it is in rising from these muddy depths that a glimmer of hope was found, and they have risen stronger, and wiser, and totally unapologetic.

With each new day a new chapter of life begins. Rewrite it your way. It's your story. You choose it. Your choices shape you into your Being. Do you take the left path or the right? Imagine the ripple effect of sharing your story, the legacy you could create by simply being you. By walking your path, your truth, every day – standing in your power, 100% totally, Unapologetically You.

I am delighted to introduce to you the following women, who today, follow their hearts with every breathe they take.

Much love,

Jennifer xx

Meet Lori Gatsi-Barnett

Having lived and worked across different cultures and countries, the richness of variety within diversity demands change from us collectively to become the examples of a community transformed and strengthened by us sharing a vision of a brighter tomorrow.

https://www.linkedin.com/in/lori-gatsi-barnett-170b5213/

https://www.facebook.com/lori.gatsibarnett

To Rise As A Phoenix

Hello world it's me! And yes, I have earned my stripes in this amazing life … Oh, but the journey and the price you must pay! The time you must spend planning, hoping, praying, simply wishing everything put on the line makes the cut. And yes, absolutely yes! you do win it all in the end. All on your own terms, unapologetically of course and delightfully you raise a glass after such an incredible roast and smile at yourself, soak in the moment, the memories and drink up because I completely understand why I am unapologetically me!

So, this me I'm talking about, she was and still is a curious little girl. Daring herself, defiant and just so darn determined to face all her fears. To become everything the world told her, she had no business wanting, had no right to claim, let alone feel that she truly deserved happiness and success together ...That whole notion was absurd! Did that stop me? No, it didn't! It challenged me to take on life's critics, motived me to striving ahead and inspired me to be the change I needed to see. This sparked a flame within me that I fight with everything I have to never let it go out. Because that flame to me is my personal reason, my source of energy, my guiding light, my secret place, my true north in my journey so far.

My mother always said be you and only you and as a child I found it odd because I didn't understand what she meant exactly until I grew up. When I left home for university no one prepared me that I was going to literally face the world in my classes and everything I thought I knew was going to be challenged. To my classmates I was different, my looks, my accent, my culture, my background and my values were to be questioned and tested. Again, as if I needed to be reminded, one of my professors said to me one day after he singled me out to speak up in the lecture, "Don't you ever apologise for being who you are, embrace it, own it and never lose sight of it!" That day uncertain of what would happen I spoke my truth to power, pretending to be confident I faked courage to fit in, in that moment and as I sat down after my speech in response to the question, only to hear him say …"Now that's the making of a true born leader who will one day change the world" He single handily silenced all my critics and empowered me for life!

In that life lesson I learnt that we all have the ability to make a difference to someone else who might need strength to face their fear in that moment. Recognising that in your own abilities lies your power to be you! It's not something you borrow or lend, not something you can trade or replace, not something that is transferable or can be shared, not something that can be copied or imitated. We are each born with abilities some of which if you never give yourself time to discover them you will always find yourself wondering, What if? Fundamentally a part of you recognises that there is something more to you but you need to figure it out for yourself... the funny thing is too often we think that the job, responsibility, money, fame, power, love, family can make you feel whole to fill this empty space you discover. You can spend your whole life committed to things that never fulfil you, leave you day dreaming, anticipating the next big thing. Surprisingly you are the biggest news headline story there ever was, but you never stopped in front of the mirror. To just stand there, notice how amazing you are, see that twinkle in your eyes as your whole face beams and you smile unapologetically and have your signature dance move take over your body as you realise it was you all along!

The key is me and quite rightfully so! When the world is such a huge space to be singled out, there is no one else in the world like me so why should I apologise for figuring myself out. Who said I had to be like anyone else when I'm the only one of my kind? How many times have you followed the crowd only to find when you thought about it ...It wasn't yours to follow anyway. When did having an opinion or view that was yours a difference to wreckon with especially since what makes you, you can't be found anywhere else. What matters most is knowing the why in the me that I really am. You see it took me some time to come to terms with understanding that loving myself was far more important than being loved by somebody else. Appreciating me with all my "flawsomeness "was the best advice I took and make a note to apply daily. Now let's face it your physical appearance will change over the years but who you are deep down inside doesn't change at all. Life will be interesting and sadly you will get some curve balls that will literally pull the rug from beneath you but you must bounce back! Keep them arms swinging because you cannot give in, the fight is not over till you win! So, hold on if you must because the ride gets bumpy and some of the turns are sharp and jagged.

Just like a superhero who knows their kryptonite you have to learn to save yourself. That's selfish you might think but realistically you owe yourself a recovery plan. Sometime set aside to think it all through. Now how we each go about hurting, resuming our individual normal is unique and as such expect nothing less when not everyone understands your actions or choices. Be brave enough to trust your instincts, walk away from things and people as unapologetically as you can. Equally not all bridges need burnt either because life has a funny way of making things come full circle and no one wants to have egg on their face surely. In my experiences so far, approach even the most difficult things with some degree of openness as nothing so far is ever really as it seems.

My next dawn occurred the day I held my baby girl in my arms for the first time. counting fingers and toes checking everything was where it was supposed to be. Those curious brown eyes looked into mine and all she could see was me. She certainly had no expectations, no ideas but the purest sincerest recognition which simply acknowledged I know you in a no pretence kind of way. Oh, the gazes, noticing everything, picking up every single expression and mimicking it back now that was something ...In that moment I was good enough, I was loveable, I was who she needed, I was unpolemically me and every day of this little girl, my number one baby girl life in my arms she would grow up to see me always and accept me. Now life doesn't get any sweeter than that right! Bring out the violins and tissues moments like this are so profound and so the making of this me! Nothing to date in my life tops that feeling and yes throughout the parenting journey oh that me is tested ...teenager now. Often seems sweet and sour, just remove the strings on the violin and no thank you for the tissues give me a mountain top so I can yell help! Because this chapter is swift and the pages just open without notice! Yes, this part is also so precious to me because that discovery is still happening and I need it just as much for me to grow and be challenged in another way, even if occasionally I'm not laughing through it unapologetically it's just the two of us and there is happiness in that!

Another fun fact you never discover till it happens is simply your life is exactly what you're happy with. You create what suits you and there is such a liberty and peace in accepting that. Whether marriage works out or you hear yourself saying irreconcilable differences, standing up for yourself can be difficult with all the judgement and do you think you can do it all by yourself? It might never be a chapter you ever have to face but it's important especially today, to not be afraid of different. You see what probably looks sad and difficult can actually be the most liberating unapologetically kindest act of loving who you choose you want to be and that certainly deserves a spa treatment weekend.

Flash back ... now between you and me we've all had the worst storm, tornado experience even. You don't talk about it at all in the beginning because you're still trying to piece together to yourself what happened ...How did you not see it coming or you made excuses for it, you lied about it, put on a brave face, hid it even, but when everyone was gone and the mask came off you had to learn how to cope with this ugly mess. You never asked for, certainly didn't deserve but it happened and you must figure it out. Whether it be grief, loss of a relationship, sickness or just that tricky time where nothing goes right and everything is wrong. No matter how hard you try this too shall pass and when you wipe away the tears, flush away the bitterness, stop blaming yourself and quit the endless ride on the emotional roller coaster. Losing my brother Lloyd was by far the hardest heart wrenching period that left me lost without him as I never got to say goodbye the way we promised. We shared a bond that was simply unbreakable, we laughed as much as we passionately argued over things and surrender! What to be called a wimp ...Never! Oh, we always held our own but never sulked beyond two seconds. You see we made a pact as kids in our back yard we vowed to always share everything we went through and be each other's rock for eternity and to no fault of his own he broke that promise. I wasn't there in the final moment and he couldn't be put on life support at the very least to allow me to fly home and let him know I was still here always like the vow. But like my brother he did keep his promise because about a month after the funeral every morning for about 2months he got my attention like he always did when we were kids. Every morning whoever got up before the other timed just how long it would take the other to wake up then use that as a means to brag over and claim dibs all day on mostly anything ...silly but it passed the time and the memories that go with it!

Now I'm no expert in what happens in the afterlife but I'm certain some allowances are made especially if there are vows to be kept, I guess. So here goes my goodbye ... I would wake up and there he was at the edge of the bed but strangely he never let me see his face and when I woke up excited, I wanted to talk so badly but all I got was seeing him there and how he shrugged his shoulders just to prove he won again. I was angry at the world for taking him and the pain of everything I wanted to tell him and have him share with me hurt so much I was just numb for the longest ...But finally I got my conversation in a dream on a long bus ride together where we talked laughed and cried like all times and just before the last stop, I had to get off the bus because I wasn't allowed till the end. Oh, I sobbed uncontrollably, held on to him as he walked me off the bus, I begged him not to leave me again because strangely I had him back and I wasn't going to give up and miss this again! To watch him get back on the bus, hear him tell me he will always be there with me till my day comes and I can be where he is, even now as I write this I'm overwhelmed by the memory. He gave me some closure and the vow were honoured and I'm convinced he must be my guardian angel and I treasure that.

After facing this loss and the years that followed, you do get that brilliant day where healing arrives! Like the phoenix you rise in all your splendour and a magnificent rebirth from the ashes from all that sadness and pain. The pain never leaves you it just becomes bearable! You wake up one morning and you know you must go on because through this dark period you equally have changed and you have to step outside and find yourself again. Remember you are breath taking, you survived to tell your story, you are alive and you certainly can own your experience unapologetically. So, you get a life makeover, in with the refreshed, vibrant and glowing you. The trick is to remain true to yourself, change is always a good thing but be patient and kind to yourself even the phoenix needs a moment to see the transformation!

Let's open the cupboard, what do we have here ...One of the hardest part of a new chapter is realising how much doesn't fit anymore. Are you the hoarding type who can't let go of anything, are you the throw it all out can't stand the sight of any of it, are you the organised will find a logical explanation for everything or are you still standing there staring not knowing where to start. Isn't it odd how you can spend your whole life with scrapbook filled with memories, carry around a suitcase filled with things, bury within yourself negative unhelpful lies that imprison you. So how do you talk yourself out of doubting, fear, uncertainty? Like they say you walk one foot in front of the other ...it's like that. What keeps you alive is not knowing everything, predicting what happens next or avoiding opening the door to see what's on the other side. Make plans sure but will they happen in the order you like, find new hobbies, travel, update everything, dare yourself to be bold and beautiful.

Unapologetically me in this very moment is so thankful. I realise that throughout my life, my family and not too many animals, belonging to you in our tribe "Gatsi Unit "has been the best! The freckle faced bouncy red head who was my best friend who lived next door, how many muddy afternoons in the yard we had so unaware of the world around us that preferred we were enemies than friends. The playgroup filled with water colours and stained aprons and all my teachers especially Ms Pollard with poise and etiquette for ballerinas you insisted on and sitting oh with grace to play the piano as you walked around the great hall watching us reciting our play lists both in the classroom and in life, people who have touched my life. there have always been so many different personalities that have influenced and inspired just the same. For that employer who made my corporate journey so empowering, by taking time to meet me on my first day as an intern, and giving me the oh so famous nickname "kid Gee" of which no matter my promotions embarrassed me always I can still see the pleasure in your face as for a while I wasn't called Lori at all. For that first kiss, that was awkwardly planted in my face in full view of what felt like the whole high school watching, boys will be boys and timing well that's another story. Then one fine day yes you finally meet, to that one you know "The One" who captures your heart for life and you will never forget. Now the most fascinating bunch of colleagues in so many walks of life, you lot are absolute legends and no matter how many years come and go the fact we are still connected decades later well you know it ...Your special people. Thank you for in your own way who I am in part needed you to be a part of story in your individual chapter.

So that's my story unapologetically me! After having written this, I feel like I've lived all over again remembering these events in my chapters. Would I change some things? Probably but what reflections would I have if I created all my chapters and there would be no room to fully become me. Looking back, I wouldn't trade any single moment! There is also such a comfort in allowing that curious girl to see what comes next as the years fly by. Knowing what I have grown to appreciate and love about the whole experience. Life is such a beautiful thing and to have an opportunity to flip through pages and smile because for a split second without notice through my memories I've embraced a history full of rich encounters that will always profoundly unlock key elements that continue to enrich who I am presently, in the future and always. Unapologetically me is a confession of my personal truth and proclamation with such excitement and anticipation of more in all the marvellous infinity of possibilities that I hope you know as you read this. I can promise you undoubtedly without question that there will be moments you will question everything and once in a while wish you had a different result. But in the meantime, simply remember what you have at your fingertips. Its adventure time, so go out there and find your *Unapologetically Me* story!

Xoxo

Lori

More about Lori

I am an entrepreneur, Motivational Speaker, and am the Founder of JoinHer Network.

I was born in Harare, Zimbabwe and lived and studied in Pennsylvania, United States. I am an Experienced Director with a demonstrated history of working in the corporate and voluntary administration industry. I am skilled in advertising, marketing strategies, business and motivational speaking and event hosting.

 I am grateful for the opportunities and my experiences arising from my work as a Youth Ambassador with World Vision and the American Red Cross. I have also participated in numerous panel discussions, including one held in the World Health Organisation's (WHO) headquarters in Geneva, Switzerland with my involvement encompassing humanitarian community building projects.

I believe, having lived and worked across different cultures and countries, the richness of variety within diversity demands change from us collectively to become the examples of a community transformed and strengthened by us sharing a vision of a brighter tomorrow.

Meet Karen Hendriks

Karen strongly believes that a child who reads will be a lifelong learner and has much greater opportunities later in life. Karen generously gives her time as an author to low socio-economic schools and communities with Indigenous literacy being her biggest passion. She believes children should read because they want too not because they have to.

https://www.linkedin.com/in/karen-hendriks-6235b356/

www.karenhendriks.com

Becoming A Shiny Happy Children's Author

When a life-threatening illness happens, you change as a person and realise that time is not always on your side. Nothing is promised. The writing dream that I'd kept hidden inside my heart started to roar loudly after a close call with death from sepsis, which is blood poisoning.

As I was fighting for my life I spilt tears of regret and cried, 'But I haven't written my picture books.' I held a deep sadness because a part of being unapologetically me wasn't being honoured.

An inner voice had been nudging me for a long time to become a children's author but I had pushed it faraway into another galaxy. As a mum and teacher, I had read loads of picture books and even dared to whisper to my students that I wanted to write but that is as far as my writing dream had gone. I was dancing with the idea of becoming a children's author but I wasn't yet ready to shine like the sun.

I often read to my students the big book Gangmangang, a local indigenous story about Windang Island. As a university student I had been involved in helping a local school create this book. To this day the book is still used in Illawarra schools. My students loved seeing my photo on the back of the book with the teachers and students involved with the project. From this experience I saw the power of own voice and story. You see, everything we do in life leads us on to new paths and new beginnings as we journey through life seeking our purpose.

I attended the University of Wollongong for my teaching degree and for a major task we had to write a short story. My lecturer and tutor made a point of writing on my story and personally finding and telling me 'You have a talent for writing and you should write.' This definitely planted a seed for my writing dream. I thought one day I will write but I don't know when. It created a big shift in my thinking. I knew that one day I would be a children's writer and that by doing this I'd be totally and unapologetically me .

The call to write can be blocked and stopped by fear and a lack of confidence. Just like *Max* in *Where the Wild Things Are* I let my inner monster's rule. I held the thought that I needed to work longer and harder so that one day I could become a children's author. Could I ever become the ruler of my dreams like Max? Yet dreams are amazing and continue to grow no matter how impossible they seem. Once they take hold there is no turning back because your soul wants you to learn to be your true self.

Little did I realise that the pursuit of something you love makes you a shiny happy person because you're honouring yourself. For me, becoming a children's author was going to achieve both happiness and well-being. However, I believed that financial security was needed first. This is true but it held me back because my focus was taken away from what would make me truly happy inside. Often our thoughts or beliefs need to change if we want to lead that joyous life that we wish upon a star for.

Let's travel back a decade, to when life was crazy busy and there was never enough time. I always seemed to be running to and from something so there wasn't any time to even imagine writing. Just like *Don't Let the Pigeon Drive the Bus* by Mo Willems I didn't say no to the pigeon. It was driving the bus really fast and my writing dreams were left far behind in its dust. I didn't allow myself time to stop and think. I was too busy running on the wheel of life. I have since learnt that a fast life is not always the best life and that most definitely a slower life is much better for me. This allows the time to listen to my heart and soul. Running away from your dreams will cause regret at some stage in your life.

The universe sent sepsis my way to set me on the path of my writing dream. As I healed, I was forced to realise what was important to me. At first, I went back to teaching but I started to voice that I was going to become a children's author. The energy for my dream grew and at one stage I was asked to teach creative writing as a relief teacher to Stage three students. I wondered how this would go as they already did an English block in the morning. It turned out to be loads of fun for all of us. I also started sharing my short stories with the junior classes. I was nudging closer to letting go of teaching which had been such an important and fulfilling part of my life. Being empowered means you need to step into your new shoes and be ready to walk in them.

One day, I finally came home and out of the blue I blurted, 'That's it, I'm done, I'm not going to teach anymore I'm going to write children's books.' My heart sure did sing when I said those words. I was starting to grow a writing voice. I didn't care that some people thought I was crazy to throw away teaching because that was their perception not mine. When I think for myself and not worry about what others think I am empowered.

Those first years at home involved a lot of soul searching. I couldn't find a writing tribe in my area and the one picture book group I did find was in a neighbouring city. The group was full and didn't want new members, so I started collecting and reading picture books and trying to write on my own. Much like the Little Red Hen I thought then I will do it myself. There will be road blocks to your goals and much like water you need to flow around them. Later I learnt that you do need writing friendships and to share your journey. Standing in your power creates positive energy as you move in flow with life.

When you try something new you have no idea how to do it and you need to find your way. I had to let go of being a teacher and how a teacher thinks and writes. A teacher's writing can be telling and a children's author definitely needs to show not tell. I had to discover how to do this but it is one thing to know this and another thing to actually be able to do it. I found this took loads of time and practise and it still does. Now, I often say to myself 'Is there too much telling in this story?' The rose-coloured glasses needed to be removed so that I could see the real bones of a story.

Continually learning and growing my picture book writing craft started to build and create confidence and self-empowerment.

I write stories on my laptop and enjoy creating them, this is the fun part of story creation for me. It is where the magic is and the place I feel the most soul alignment. I love creating a story about something that calls me from my heart. Then the real work begins with the editing of a story over and over again. Often a story is edited hundreds of times because each word in a picture book has to count and earn its place. My first picture book Go Away, Foxy Foxy, was worked on for four years over and over again. Editing is a skill that evolves and grows and it takes a long time to learn. This involves critique groups, assessments and loads of patience. An empowered woman realises the value of a friendship network and working towards her goals.

Often fear is created by judgement of yourself and your abilities. I had a limiting self-belief in my head. *Who am I to write a picture book?* I found my truth in creating my words. I learnt that each word that I wrote made me a better writer. I decided to keep my journey real and authentic and to try not to judge myself about my writing journey and to just accept it and do it. Recognising that you have what it takes and activating it is honouring your strengths not your weaknesses.

One of the biggest ways to do this was by not comparing my writing journey to others. You may wish for their success as some people rise to the top quickly and for others it's a slow burn. But when I judge my writing and my abilities my energy drops and my thoughts darken. I feel hurt, insecure, inadequate and vulnerable. I choose not to judge myself and be strong and confident and empowered.

One of the biggest lessons writing has taught me is to develop self-love and that the journey is much more important thing than the destination. Success will come in its own time. Being a writer leads to much soul work as you draw from within. If you chose to write to feel special or smart or enough, you will never be satisfied and continually judge yourself and your writing. I am continually working on what is deep down inside I know that my writing is my reward. I can write. It's empowering just saying that isn't it?

It took a while but I did gather the courage to join a critique group and this helped to hone my editing skills and made me become accountable. I could see holes in other people's stories and I loved giving feedback. It was easy to do this for others but I was often blinded to the flaws in my own stories. This is why we all need each other. You will often hear let a story sit and at the beginning I would be so in love with a story that I didn't do this. It's embarrassing when I look back at a story that was forced or cooked too quickly. This children's writing game is one of patience and it sure is a slow burn thing. An empowered woman recognises the value of patience and support.

One of the hardest lessons I had to learn was to know when to leave a group and move on when it no longer works for you. Making difficult decisions can be confronting but I did leave a critique group. It was a hard thing to do because I adored the members but we were not posting stories often enough and I wanted more consistency. The group posted a mix of middle grade and picture book stories. My focus was picture book stories so I left and have since joined another group that only focuses upon picture book stories. My heart is lighter, happier and fuller. As the saying goes – trust your instincts.

One of the first supportive places that I did discover was Creative Kids Tales on Facebook. I would read the posts and over the years I slowly started to join in the conversations and the online community. I have since joined other forums and found that the more I became a part of the writing community the more authentic I feel. This fosters a sense of belonging. The writing world is quite small but it is supportive and if you make the effort others make the effort too. Empowered people take strength from each other.

The first conference I ever attended was KidLit in Victoria, as I walked in the door I was overwhelmed and felt like an imposter. I was emitting a low energy vibration. Everyone seemed to know someone, I timidly watched, took notes and soaked it all up. I wondered how do I fit in? This was a whole new world with lots of shiny baubles. I did learn that people were friendly and polite but it was still rather lonely. It would be this way until I found my place and owned it. You see, you have to believe in you and what you do and then make a commitment to it. This attracts positive energy and moves you forward in pursuit of your goals.

One of the first things I did do was submit a short story for an anthology not really thinking anything would happen with it and I was so surprised to see it accepted and published. I won a picture book competition in 2017 and this really boasted my confidence. You see, picture book writing takes loads of time and effort. Each day, I would walk to a local coffee shop and write something. Sometimes I would catch up with my friends and share a story and they were always so kind and encouraging. They could see how important my writing dream was to me. What I didn't know is that lots of people in my local community could see me chipping away at my dream and that I was inspiring them with my passion and determination. Everything you do has a ripple effect in the world for we are all parts of one big whole. Being empowered encourages others.

Still, sharing with my friends wasn't going to develop my writing craft but it did build my confidence. I went about my writing journey with much more bravery and resilience. By living and speaking my truth I was starting to evolve as a writer and person.

I kept chipping away at developing my writing craft and decided if I couldn't find my writing tribe I would create my one, so I did. Shellharbour Children's Writers and Illustrators was born. I originally planned on meeting once a week but the six members loved it so much that we would meet weekly. However, once again I had become the teacher and was busily helping others achieve their dreams. I was attending conferences and doing workshops and sharing all my knowledge. After two years and due to Covid I stopped the group but gained some wonderful friendships and perhaps one day I will start it again as the area really needs a group like this. But for now, I am continuing to learn and grow myself first. This taught me that sometimes you do need to put yourself first and that it's okay to do this.

Something that really did make me feel like a children's author was to attend the Sunshine Writers Retreats. Here I was with like-minded creatives and I made my first true writing friendships. I attended the retreats for three years with the same wonderful group of friends who are now my heart writer friends. We don't share manuscripts but we do connect often and share writer friendship, love and support. I am grateful that I had the opportunity to do these retreats because I finally felt like I belonged and that I was a children's writer. You can't do everything on your own and writer friendships are terribly important. Writer friendships become the wind beneath your wings.

One of the biggest ways to create overall happiness and well-being is your relationships, the people around you – family, friends and significant others. I was fortunate that my partner and friends could see how terribly important my writing was to me and my internal happiness. The third part of the triangle was my writing friendships. My happiness triangle was now complete. To be empowered we need to feel loved and supported.

Writing held a great significance and gave me a renewed purpose in life. This sense of purpose was very important to my well-being and happiness. My happiness came from how my writing made me feel and the well-being came from the contentment of doing something that I loved.

Writing children's stories involves lots of rejection so remaining optimistic and staying resilient is so important. I celebrate any successes no matter how big or small they are and savour and appreciate each one. I celebrate personalized rejection letters and take all the positives out of any feedback that I receive. I know that the market is flooded with books and I choose not to take rejections personally, because first and foremost it's a commercial market. My writing may sing but that doesn't mean it suits the current market or a publishers list. I choose to remain optimistic and hopeful and take the greatest pleasure from each story as it is moving me forward and making me a better writer.

My successes started off small and slowly built. I submitted short stories to anthologies and they were the first place that my stories were published. This not only boosted my confidence but my writers CV. It enabled me to meet the most wonderful and inspiring women whose kindness has been an important part of my writing journey. By giving and receiving kindness I have bloomed. Upon reflection, two amazing women included in this anthology, Jennifer Sharp and Michelle Worthington have been my kindness angels on my author journey. I am grateful to have them in my life. They're my superheros. Do seek the support of writer experts and give support to others in return. Then the possibilities are endless.

A mentor is a trusted guide with expertise and a constructive mentoring relationship can be life-changing for a writer. Whether you dip into a mentoring relationship for a short period or a little longer they will help you rethink and focus. Both parties can reap the rewards and learn and grow. Someone who actively listens and gives constructive feedback gives you courage to move forward and grow. I have been mentored and I too have helped others in return. What goes around comes around.

Don't take yourself to seriously and enjoy all those writer moments of joy. Surprising positives can be found and taken from each writer day. One way that I do this is by writing quotes on Instagram. I wait until I have inspiration and then I capture it and share it. I read children's books and get lost in the type of books that I want to write. You see, the more I read the more I grow. As a reading specialist I taught reading and writing together, one could not go without the other. This is also true as a children's author, read what you want to write.

Oops, one of the things that I have always intuitively known is to use what you know and don't pretend to know what you don't. In my stories there is always a part of me in each one and this makes my voice authentic and real. Life isn't those perfect Instagram moments and there will be down moments but I choose to bounce back. The ups and downs of life are always going to be there. It's how you react to them that counts.

I'm invested in my writing journey and the children's publishing industry is continually evolving and changing so I know that I need to keep on learning, changing and moving forward. Being invested in what you do empowers you and keeps you moving forward and not becoming stuck.

When I was recovering from sepsis I read Eckhart Tolle's *The Power of Now*. This book helped me immensely and was part of my spiritual healing. All that any of us really have is the now so I'm so glad that I found my joy. Find what makes you a shiny, happy person. Little did I realise that my journey on becoming a children's author would teach me how to live an empowered life and to be joyously and totally me.

More about Karen

Karen is an Australian picture book author and literacy specialist. A full-time writer based on the south coast of New South Wales, Karen writes from the heart, is curious and imaginative. Her inspiration comes from nature, travel, family and her love of coffee and a chat. She has a wealth of experience as a primary school teacher and has an extensive picture book library at home. Karen prefers to read children's books rather than adult books.

The international Rubery Book Awards shortlisted Karen's picture book Feathers in 2021. Her Sudeten German heritage inspired her picture book Home, which is listed on the Australian Refugee Council's webpage as a picture book resource. Go Away, Foxy Foxy is used in local schools as a teaching resource for its great language and story. Karen regularly appears at charity events for children and is a Books in Homes Ambassador. She is active within her community with story time sessions and hosted a story rock challenge in her local village. During the recent online Global Learning Festival Karen hosted story time with an international audience.

Karen strongly believes that a child who reads will be a lifelong learner and has much greater opportunities later in life. Reading creates confidence and makes you happy inside. It has been her passion as a teacher and now as an author to foster a love of reading in all children. Karen generously gives her time as an author to low socio-economic schools and communities. Indigenous literacy is one of Karen's biggest passions. She believes working collaboratively with others with the same passion creates the change you wish to see, which is children who read because they want too not because they have to.

Meet Robin Ross

Each one of my wrinkles reminds me that I have had a great life. I have loved, lost, hugged, cried, travelled, made great friends, lost friends, made stupid mistakes and still I am ok.

https://www.linkedin.com/in/robindjkuipers/

www.pumptpt.com.au

Perfectly Imperfect

I put my foot down lightly on the breaks of my car; in the distance I could just make out flashing red and blue lights through the dark Johannesburg night. I slowed down hoping that whoever was involved in whatever had occurred ahead was okay.

I could feel a slight pull on the wheel as I drove over some of the gravel that had spilled into the road from the building sites lining the road. I could feel my car starting to gently slide towards the median, I tried to counter - steer but in an instant, I lost complete control. The tyre of my car caught in the rut at the side of the road that had been dug out to stop the gravel from spilling onto the road acted like a catapult and sent my car rocketing onto the opposite side of the freeway.

The dark of the night invaded the safety of the car. They say your life flashes in front of your eyes when you are. in a position of crisis – all I was thinking was fuck! My baby! Please dear God please let my baby be okay. There was silence, a deafening silence as I slowly opened my eyes and fuzzy outlines slowly started to clear; the sound of whimpering pulling me out of my daze. I Lay halfway out of the front windscreen, pulling myself out of my car that was now upside down on its roof, pain shooting through my whole body and blood dripping into my eye, My baby Jo was lying in her car chair, on its side, still buckled in, head lolling to one side, tiny whimpers of 'mummy, mummy, mummy' coming out of her little rosebud mouth. Her little face with her little rosy cheeks flawless; her eyes closed as if sleeping and just her faint plea for me to swoop in to save her.

Something happened. Something in my head just snapped and I moved with lightning speed unclasping the seat belt and whipping my baby out of the chair. I ran. I ran like I had never run before. I knew there were people that could help just down the road. I had remembered seeing them just before I lost control of my car. Everything that we learn about not moving someone after an accident went out the window. My concern was to find someone to save my baby, to wind back time so I would make different choices; wind back time so I could change my reactions.

I saw people running towards me as I bolted up the median strip. I once again saw those blue and red flashing lights. I saw what looked like saviours. As two running forces collided someone whipped Jo from me and started calling into a radio, another grabbed me and was shouting - shouting so loud, 'what happened? What happened?' All I could say was, 'Where is my baby?'

In a flurry of people, sounds, shouting and movement, I gathered that they had air lifted my precious child to the hospital. She was critical. I shouted. I screamed. I begged to go with her. They said, 'No. I was to go in the ambulance, and we would meet her at the hospital.' I lashed out and I swore at the idiot that thought I would let them take her without me. I felt a prick in my arm and slowly a warm, soft, and quiet light enveloped me. All my fight was gone. I descended into darkness. That was my last recollection of the accident.

I came to on a hospital bed in Johannesburg General Hospital – bright lights overhead, the soft shoes of doctors and nurses squeaking; the lyrical beep of machines. I sat bolt upright instinctively knowing that I needed to go and find my baby. I grabbed a handful of hospital sheets, realising that my shirt had been cut from my body, got off the bed and walked down the emergency corridor opening all of the curtains as I went. At last, I came across my precious three-year-old lying on a bed with pipes dangling out of her mouth, needles in her arm - these being the only indication that she was not sleeping peacefully.

The resident doctor, nurse, whoever was there quickly turned and informed me in a very authoritarian voice, that I was not allowed in the cubicle. I looked at her and I swear if looks could kill she would have died right there. By the look on my face, I think she realised who I was and softened, she put out her hand and invited me in to sit with Jo, to hold her little chubby hand; to run my fingers through her golden hair. I touched her soft baby skin. It was so smooth and perfect. What had happened? How was I sitting here watching my baby fight for her life?

The next few days was lived in a blur - a blur of doctors, no sleep and worry. I'm not a religious person but I bargained. I bargained like I have never bargained before. I promised that I would be a better person and go to church. I promised to never take anyone for granted. I bargained my life for Jo's. I wanted to take her place. I had lived, loved, adventured, and experienced so much. She was only three. Then I got angry and swore at God - why would he do this to a baby? Where was this all-loving entity? I cried. I am not sure words could describe the emotions that I felt. With every blip on her machine, it instilled hope. With every eye movement, I would imagine this event being something we discussed as we got older.

The time came when Jo gave up. I remember the day so clearly, even twenty-five years later. Her nurse, who happened to also be called Jo, asked me if I wanted to hold her while she changed the sheets. I gently lifted her and cradled her in my arms, hugging her close, so close, barely being able to hear or feel her heartbeat. I never wanted to let go. I smelt her baby smell. I felt her rhythmic breathing. I gentle placed my finger in her fat little morphine laden fist. I felt the tiniest squeeze as she closed her little hand over my finger – Oh, dear God, the first reaction from her since the accident. Was this a sign that she was on the mend? Before I could start rejoicing, the steady blip that I heard turned into a solid drone. Her fight was over. She could hang on no more.

My world stopped right there. I have no idea how long I sat there for. Everyone and everything ceased to exist. There was nothing left for me to feel. The nurse Jo brought me back to reality. 'Robin,' she said, 'Jo is gone. I know that this is not a great time, but she could save so many other people with her organs, would you consider?' There was no hesitation. Jo, at three, was the most incredible little human and I know that she would have wanted to give what she could so that someone else would not have to go through what we had to go through. I reluctantly let them take her and I was left alone and numb.

Losing a child is not the natural order of things, no parent should have to bury a child, and me barley twenty-three years old, a child myself, I was unable to even process what had happened.

A week later I sat in the church watching four grown men carry a 53cm white coffin with the remains of my baby cradled in white satin. I maintained my composure through the service and even managed to make it through the wake. I smiled and nodded through the 'God, only takes the best flowers for his garden,' and the 'she is in a better place now,' and even had an individual say, 'It's okay, you are still young, and you will have more kids.' What the...! I now know that people do not generally know how to react to grief and will say what they feel will soothe and unburden the person experiencing the loss. Truthfully, I wanted to punch quite a few people and would have preferred to sit quietly with my baby and say my final farewells.

What do you do after something like this? I went shopping. Not the usual exciting, fun-filled, giggle laden shopping that Jo and I had done. It was a solemn, sad, and empty trudge around shops filled with parents shouting at their children to hurry, getting impatient with them for lagging behind, shouting at them for spilling their juice or not wanting to stay in their pram; everyday shit that I would have given my life to experience one last time. I sat in the busy food court of Eastgate Shopping Centre and ordered a coffee. As I sat, I reflected on life, events that had bought me to sitting in a shopping centre feeling like I had just killed my baby.

I grew up in an unconventional family, a mother and father that travelled extensively as they were the quintessential 60's hippies. Free loving, leather working, surfing, drug taking hippies with a zest for life. We travelled extensively. My brother being born in Mauritius and me being born in Australia and settling in South Africa for the duration of my childhood. What I can remember growing up was great. A big house close to the beach, two Afghan hounds, a goat and a few chickens. Long walks to the beach, octopus hunting, playing outside with my brother running around sun-kissed, not a care in the world.

My little word was shattered when my real dad decided that he no longer wanted to hang around; being a free spirit and a skipper by trade, he felt bogged down by two small children and a wife. He had so much to still do with his life and we were obviously an encumbrance. He left. My mum was incredible when he took flight and before long, we didn't really worry about not having a dad, our days were once again filled with animals, beach, and sunshine.

My mother met up with a guy that was a DJ. When my brother and I were about five and six, her new relationship changed our lives forever. She was immediately smitten and completely engrossed. To be honest, I do not remember a great deal from this part of my life, except that we ended up moving away from the beach to a nice little suburb in Johannesburg. My father – this is what we shall call this human for the duration of this story – was now my official stepdad. He now had a good job – no more Djing and we had money. Sadly, we were no longer sun-kissed, running around naked with all our animals. We now went to school and had a routine and chores.

I reminisced as I sat alone in the noise of the shopping centre thinking back to when I was little and wondered if it was a place I wanted to go considering that I was sitting here nursing a cup of coffee after saying goodbye to my dead child. Was I in the right head space to delve into my past? Yes, I wanted to torture myself. I wanted to face all of my demons; push myself over the edge. I deserved to suffer. I wanted to feel, feel anything. At the moment, I felt dead - as dead as my baby.

It all started off with father taking me to work one day. He was a used car salesman, and I was told that it was father/daughter day. I was excited! The reason I was so excited is that father never really paid my brother and I any attention unless it was to polish his shoes, make the bed, clean the garden, mow the lawn, or move rocks from one side of the garden to the other and then back again. Let me explain. Father never had children of his own and now having two little humans in his life that he quickly found out would do his bidding with little to no argument based purely on fear of a whipping, made him a very hard and unloving parent. Saturday mornings we were woken early and depending on how he was feeling, one of us would be in his sights the whole day and the day would be manufactured to be a misery - anything we did or said was wrong and he pointed out how stupid and inadequate we were. The 'chosen one' as we affectionally termed the unfortunate one, would get the worst of the abuse, the worst of the tongue lashing, the brunt of the leather belt, his words that would stay with us forever.

So, you can imagine my excitement when I was chosen one day to attend work, grown up work with the master. Although my brother and I were close, any reprieve from the constant barrage of anger and degradation was a welcome thought. A juvenile mind does not have the capacity to understand the extent of evil in a person but does understand self-preservation.

We stayed at work a bit later on this day as father was the manager, so he had to lock up the show room. While he was finishing off, he asked me to come over and sit on his lap. I was hesitant at first, this was really a first. I did as I was told. He rubbed my back and slowly slid his hand up my skirt. I could feel something get hard underneath me. He groaned. I crawled off and looked at him horrified. Father cupped my little face and told me what a pretty little girl I was and if I was really good, he would buy me a pony. I was so scared yet excited by this. Could you imagine me having a horse? The proviso was, however, that I was to keep this 'our little secret', and as I was always so good at doing what I was told, I said nothing. Little secrets are funny things - they are sinfully fun as you feel special that you share something that no one else knows about and as you get older, you start to realise that there may be a more sinister meaning behind them.

Our secret carried on for many years and it never really dawned on me that we were any different to any other family. My stepfather used to smoke pot, so we presumed that we were never allowed to have friends over to play or stay. After all, how would he chill in his underpants watching TV smoking his pipe or joint if there were a myriad of little humans running around, right?

Our house was very unconventionally middle class dysfunctional; from the outside we looked like a successful family. Mum owned her own landscaping business all the while hiding a whiskey bottle under the front seat of her Ute to drown her unhappiness with life, a career- focused father who was extremely successful and heralded as the 'Best in the Business' by his fellow workers and industry, all the while smoking pot, snorting coke and emotionally and physically abusing his stepchildren. No one ever knew and no one ever suspected. We were required to clean the house after school every day, polish shoes and get our uniforms washed and ready for the next day and prep supper before mum got home to prepare it. Squeeze in after school sport and homework and it would be classed as a normal strict upbringing, except when these things were not done and we were disciplined, it was with an instrument called the 'persuader', a mini cricket bat, with a cute and funny poem imprinted on it about how a wife was to use the persuader on her husband if he was late from work, drank too much or whatever other shit people thought was a funny reason to hit someone. It always struck me as strange that adults had 'novelty' gifts that encouraged violence.

Our beatings were never done out of emotion, there was never a sudden slap or whipping. Father would stand us in front of him while he presided on his couch, staring at us, looking from one to the other; his huge frame, white, bare, and calm. He would simply glare at us, my brother once referred to them as black pig eyes, all the while never saying a word. He would then choose who would be the one to get the whipping and he would make the other watch. We would have to bend over his knee, and he would lift the 'persuader' high above his head and whip down on our little bums, always on naked bums. The sting would be extreme and sometimes he missed his spot and got us on the lower back or at the top of the legs. I remember wanting to run up and grab his hand as he walloped my brother, but I was too scared. Brother took so many whips for me, always the first to step up and take the blame; he was the perfect big brother.

There was one particular night we were all in the lounge. My brother and I were sitting on the floor where we were usually positioned. We were not permitted to sit on the couches - that was reserved for my little sister, mum, and father only. Father had a tin of favourites chocolates and was digging for the best for my sister. She picked up a toffee and threw it back in the tin, declaring that she did not like them. Father picked it up, whistled at brother and I and threw it at us like we were dogs. It landed squarely on my lap. I glared at him, he pointed his chubby finger at me and said, 'you should be grateful that you even get one, you little shit!' Sister laughed and said, 'Yes Robby, you are so ungrateful!' I could not stand it and got up and started to walk towards her. I intended to smack her. Father interceded, picked me up and threw me across the lounge. I connected with the fireplace, face first. There was blood all over the place. I had broken my nose. He abused me for making a mess and I was told to clean it up immediately. My brother once again came to my aide and tried to help me clean up 'my mess.'

The happy façade all came crashing down when I was about sixteen and I plucked up the courage to tell my grandmother about my little 'secret' after a particularly bad beating from father. My amazing grandmother almost lost her false teeth! In a flurry of police, child protection units and lawyers, I found myself being prepped for a court case against the man I had called father for the better part of my young life. Never did I imagine that my honest chat with my grandmother would alter life for so many people in such a short space of time.

Did I feel guilty? Yes, I did. I felt guilty because my mum was accused of being removed and uninvolved because she did not have a clue what was going on. I felt guilty because my little sister, a product of my stepfather and mother was now having to deal with a father that was accused of sexually molesting a stepdaughter and I felt guilty because my brother, who had the hardest upbringing now had to deal with even more crap in his life.

The most sobering memory I have of the ordeal, was when we had our initial meeting or hearing with the authorities when fathers lawyer began to ask me questions. This was South Africa in the 1980's so the whole child protection - victim protection thing that is forefront in today's courts did not exist in any way or form at that time. This little rat of a human, the lawyer, stood in front of me and asked me - 'So, Robin, Did you ever tell anyone about what your stepfather allegedly did to you prior to talking to your granny or are you just upset because you were disciplined? Did you attempt to scream or call out to your mum, brother, or sister, when he allegedly visited you at night? Did you report your father to the authorities before this, or did you in fact enjoy it and want it to happen, in fact, instigate it, and therefore you never acted on the alleged abuse?

I sat there stunned, I had never really thought about it like that. Did I enjoy it? Is that why I never said anything? Was I the one that was doing wrong and leading my father on? Was I willing him to visit me every night? At sixteen I had never felt such doubt, self-loathing, and confusion before. I just sat there stunned and silent.

It was a long-drawn-out case that eventually came to an end. Child molestation cases are apparently hard to prove as it is a 'he said, she said' issue with very little to no evidence and notoriously difficult to get a conviction, however, father was charged with child misconduct, fined and that was the end. Well, almost the end, he was asked to leave his lucrative job and had to leave the state as an amazing court reporter got hold of the story and wrote an article, albeit a small one that landed in the newspaper. That was my last contact with him for several years. Our little family was thrust into turmoil. My mum became an alcoholic, basically lost everything and we ended on the streets. My sister ended up being sent to my stepfather as my mother was unable to look after her and my brother - I'm not too sure what he was doing. We all just scattered like paper in the wind. I always did wonder though if my stepfather ever visited the other kids.

I met the first love of my life – whom we shall name Number 1 in this story. After I'd finished school, while working in a restaurant, he was the epitome of everything I wanted in a partner – tall, long flowing locks, funny, caring, attentive and an incredibly good soul, a human from a good family. Long story short, I fell pregnant when I was eighteen and gave birth to our beautiful baby girl just before my nineteenth birthday.

My pregnancy was not a particularly difficult one - I will admit the pressures of pregnancy was different back then. I was armed with my Dr Spock book and read up on all the milestones and expectations, ensuring that I did everything just right. On January 12, 1993 I gave birth to Baby Jo as she was affectionately called – a bouncing healthy baby girl weighing 2.6kg and just the dinkiest little human I had ever laid eyes on. I know most parents will understand when I say that there is something that just clicks when you hold your little creation for the first time and the overpowering love that you have is indescribable. Everything is perfect, everything. Jo was the light in my life, my reason for living. I worried that I would end up like my parents and abuse or hurt her unintentionally. She had colic for the first six months of her little life and she simply would not sleep - I had no idea what colic was or that she had it. I used to cry in the shower thinking that I sucked as a mum, that I couldn't stop her from crying, that I was neglectful and simply an unfit mother. The number of times that I wanted to shake her until she stopped crying was countless, which only exacerbated the feelings of inadequacy.

I knew however that I would not treat my baby as I was treated. She would be cherished, loved and worshiped as the gift that she was. I remember one day my brother came to visit after a particularly long bout of crying and lifted her up, put her in the kangaroo pouch, and in a heartbeat the child fell into a deep sleep. I felt even worse about myself.

Overall, though, Jo was perfect, perfect in every way. She was this little blonde-haired, blue-eyed angel, with a quick wit and a great sense of humour - everyone always commented that she was an 'old soul' and she proved to be just that. Taken way too soon. The sound of a child screaming pulled me out of my reminiscing. A mother was screaming at her child for spilling a milkshake on the floor of the food court in the shopping centre. The child was crying, snot dripping out of his nose and tears sprouting out of his little eyes. I looked at the scene unfolding in front of me and wondered how she would feel if she knew she only had him for a short space of time, that life was so fragile and, in an instant, he could be gone, would the spilt milkshake mean that much?

After Jo's funeral I found myself still getting up in the morning making two cups of tea, one for me, one for her, running her bath in the afternoon, and walking into her room to turn down her covers on her bed at night. I had to get out of the house, away from everything and everyone. Growing up the way I did, drugs were a natural part of my life, and it was in them that I sought solace and comfort. Five years passed in a haze of nights out, drunken and drug fuelled parties. I wanted to die, I wanted not to be here without Jo. Nothing filled the gap, in fact I wanted nothing to fill the gap, I wanted to make myself suffer, hurt, and feel.

I will never forget the day that everything changed for me. It was after a particularly hectic three-day bender, I managed to drag my sorry 45kg arse out of bed and walked into the bathroom to splash my face. On my twenty first birthday Jo had bought me a gold chain, that Number 1 had organised, bless his cotton socks, which until her death I never took off. When she passed and I packed everything away, I put this chain away too, for safe keeping. On this particular day, after splashing my face I lifted the towel off the rack and there hanging under the towel was her chain. I had just finished taking enough drugs to sink the titanic. It was just hanging there. And in this lies the miracle –I thought I had packed it away for safe keeping and then there it was! I do not know how it got there – divine intervention perhaps, me putting it there in a drunk or drugged stupor – perhaps?

I fell to my knees, and I cried, deep, gut-wrenching tears, five years of pain, anguish and sorrow all came out at the same time. The emptiness inside seemed to disappear and the need to get my act together was so very strong. It was a long road, I got better, I fell again, I got up again. I tried and I failed but eventually I clawed my way out of the black, dark space and I could finally see the light and it was not that of a freight train coming straight at me.

I then met an incredible man, who shall be known as 'Absolutely Incredible' to protect his true identity. He was five years younger than me chronologically but probably fifty years older than me in attitude and outlook. Ask him what he wanted out of life, and his answer simply 'was to be happy!' A new life opened for me, and I felt that I no longer had to feel sad. I felt I could smile again, feel happy again. He made me realise that I was to celebrate the years that I had with Jo and not mourn the years that I did not have with her. He taught me that I was so much stronger than I thought I was. What happened to me in the past was left in the past. It was there to shape me and not define me. My new adventure had begun. I realised that I would not live life in honour of my daughter; that I would live my own life, clutching onto her memory.

We moved to England from South Africa to start a new and exciting chapter for both of us, and it is at this stage - the tender age of twenty-nine - that I decided that I would follow my dream and study law. So, between experiencing London, working in restaurants, and studying, I managed to make it through my degree. One of the requirements of my qualification was to attend meetings with barristers and clients to discuss their cases. I remember on so many occasions the barristers that I worked with, rolled their eyes and let out exasperated sighs when I would bring up client's upbringings, their histories and why I felt that they did what they did. I was reminded on a regular basis that these people were there because of choices, and as they made the choices they were to deal with the consequences. I couldn't argue with this, but I do believe that good people make stupid choices but that does not make them bad people. Decisions are made based on your character, personality, and the environment in which you were raised. I realised then how powerful your environment was in shaping your future. It was then that I also realised that through my young life, being groomed by my father that, I had to do stuff to get recognition and love, was simply not enough to get love for who I was.

I remember my mum telling me one day, 'Robby, only pretty people get breaks in life, the rest have to be clever, so my girl, make sure you study hard and apply yourself.' When I tell people this they cringe, not believing that a mother would say that to her daughter. I took it as preparation for life. She could either pussy foot around the fact that I am not a conventional beauty or prepare me to accept what I look like and how society discriminates. I was a particularly good athlete in my younger years and excelled in track with hopes and dreams of being an Olympic athlete someday. All my coaches echoed these sentiments and trained me for just that. When I left primary school to attend high school, father found a school that did not offer athletics as he felt that it would not pay my rent one day. He felt I should concentrate on my academics. Basically, the words of my mother echoes in the actions of father.

My healing and years of reflection started, and some were awe-inspiringly motivating and others incredibly destructive. Some days I woke up and thought I could conquer the world and others I would feel like that scared little girl hiding from her stepdad and looking at herself in the mirror with self-loathing because she was not pretty. I would laugh sometimes when I had a moment between my busy life to think that this kind of nonsense should be something you go through at sixteen not thirty-five. The fact that at this stage of my life I still did not know what I wanted to be when I grew up, the fact that I was constantly searching for my peace, searching for where I belong, my tribe was exhausting; I never did fit in. Absolutely Incredible and I, funnily enough, never used the word 'Love.' Our term for affection or endearment was 'I like you' - simple and effective. I believe for both of us this was our way of being safe. The only time we said 'I love you' to each other was the day we got married. We eventually moved from England, back to South Africa after I graduated to be close to family. Being home for five years and some traumatic incidents (for another story) we decided that it was no longer safe to remain in the country and decided to return to my country of birth - Australia.

I was a difficult person to live with through all these changes; the constant ups and downs and positivity and then plunging into a dark and sad place. My escape was to be busy, busy working, busy growing businesses, busy with clients, busy with study, busy with events, retrospectively the 'busy' was so that I never had a moment to stop, appreciate, think, digest and analyse the driving factors behind who I was and where I was going.

In 2018 while running our personal training business, I started prepping for the Arnold Classic - the biggest body building competition in the world, and under the expert guidance of Absolutely Incredible Man won, along with many other bodybuilding competitions, and gained a few national and international records at powerlifting, all the wins, the accolades, the awards, keeping me focused and busy.

The health and wellness industry is a peculiar one - we hide behind the latest hashtags about body positive, healthy balance, intuitive eating and all the other crap that socials shovel at us. At the essence of it is body image, how we look and how wonderful we seem to other people. I fell into that trap, hook, line, and sinker. I worked extremely hard to get a fabulous body at the age forty-four. The washboard abdominal muscles, the perfect butt and a body that turned heads wherever I went. My mum and father were right. Looks get you places. I worked, I achieved, I did something, and I was rewarded by the love that I needed and craved to feel whole. It was for the comments, the likes, the shares on social media. I still felt empty, after all this time, even with this incredible human at my side and all the love pouring in through my social media accounts. My Absolutely Incredible Man was the most patient, loving, understanding and content person to my frantic, busy, goal orientated personality. It was not meant to be unfortunately and after seventeen years together, we called it quits.

Thankfully he found himself a woman that appreciates and loves him for who he is and treasures him as he should be. We have a truly unique relationship, both of us decided that there would be no bad vibes, no fighting. After spending such a long time together, we would always share the best memories of travelling, laughing, loving, crying, growing companies, selling companies, way too much to simply wipe away because we were no longer compatible. Both, he, and his partner remain great friends to me, and I treasure them like family.

My life then surprisingly, took a bit of a 360-degree turn. Being a powerlifter and training a team to compete, I attended several competitions, and it was at one of these events that I bumped into a rather spectacular man. I was not aware how spectacular he was as yet; he would be my future husband. Soul Mate was the MC at one of the comps on ANZAC day and he approached me while I was busy with my athletes and asked me if I could send him a video I had taken of him reciting the ANZAC ode. I apparently turned around and snapped at him because I was busy working. See what was happening again? Soul Mate contacted me via messenger a few days later and I obliged and sent through the video that he wanted. I gave him no more thought but after me posting something on my Facebook feed about baby Jo, I received a message from him with some beautiful, heartfelt words of support.

This was the beginning of my new life. My life the last three years has been vastly different from the last forty-four years. After years of searching, I have found my family. I have found who I want to be and where I want to go. I found my soul mate who is my grounding force, and true love. What makes my life with him different? How do I know he is my soul mate? Because he does not complete me; he compliments me. We don't need each other; we want each other. We don't like each other; we love each other. He accepts me, my past, and still wants to be part of my future. He makes me feel like the most important person in his world. Soul Mate - once again a name chosen to protect his identity is a solo dad to a beautiful daughter, Bubs. At times I must pinch myself to know that what I have is real. I have an amazing man in my life and a daughter. My family is complete. Between the two of them they have taught me to let go of the busy and live in the now. Enjoy the mornings together in pj's, drinking coffee. The three of us all huddled in our bed. They have taught me to throw away all pretences and find my inner child. We go to waterparks, we visit zoos, we picnic, we build forts, we chase each other around the backyard with the hose. We laugh at stupid cartoons, we go shopping and buy nothing, we eat fish and chips on the floor in front of TV. All the simple things in life are the things that give me the most pleasure. It is not what we do but it's because we do it together that makes it right. Bubs and Soul Mate are not replacements for my earlier family; they are my reward to getting through the pain and loss - the anguish, and the growth to become the human I am today.

They have taught me that if words can control me, this means that everyone can control me. True power is being able to sit back and observe things with logic and respond with restraint. I now breathe and allow things to pass.

I always thought of myself as fiercely independent but with them I have learnt that the inability to accept support from others is a trauma response. You know that 'I don't need anyone; I can do it myself' is an extreme survival tactic. This response is a shield that protects your heart against neglect, abuse, betrayal, and disappointment. For me it was me feeling like my parents abandoned me, my partner offering me intimacy and not honouring my heart, friendships and family who have taken more than they ever give, all the situations where people have told me that 'we are in this together', or 'I've got your back' and simply left me to pick up the pieces. I learned that if you don't put yourself in these situations, you will not be disappointed. Extreme independence is a pre-emptive strike against heartbreak, so it's simple not to trust anyone; in fact, you don't even trust yourself to choose the right people.

No matter how you dress it up and proudly display your independence the truth is that you are wounded, scarred, and broken. It is easier to hide behind your protective wall. No hurt gets in but sadly no love gets out. Thankfully, I let down my guard long enough to let in my soul mate. My life lessons have contributed to how I run my personal training business based in a tiny town about 80 kilometres out of Melbourne. When someone trains with me, we go through the obligatory discussion about goals, and I hear the hashtag answers of healthy lifestyle and better health. But in essence, 99.9% of women I train initially want to look good and I am not here to persuade them otherwise. Our work starts with them owning their motivation; together we realise that motivation changes and morphs as we change and morph. When we lie to ourselves about what we want, be it in life, love, work or spiritually, we create a destructive, toxic relationship with ourselves. If we cultivate an honest relationship, we can set realistic goals and slowly the realisation that you are able to do and be so much more becomes clearly apparent. It's not vanity to feel you have a right to be beautiful. Women are taught to feel that we're not good enough, that we must live up to someone else's standards. But my aim for my clients is for them to cherish themselves for who they are. Someone's opinion does not need to become their reality. We are proud of who and what we are - we are proud of what we stand for and fight for what we believe.

Billion-dollar industries exist to tell us that we need to be more, weigh less, and be that number. Lifting weights gives us confidence from within. Life is a journey and there is no road map. When you realise you are returning to old habits, don't be annoyed, realise that by being aware of the repeat behaviour is in fact a sign of progress. Self-awareness is key to change. My aim is to prove to all my clients that they are worthy of love; they are worthy to be cherished. They are worthy to be accepted and they are worthy to be adored. You don't have to earn it, prove it, bargain for it, or beg for it because you are worth it. A satisfied life is better that a successful life because success is measured by others and satisfaction is measured by your heart, mind and soul. Your life is your signature creation.

I don't like the stretch marks on my boobs, but they are from where I lovingly breastfed my baby that I no longer have. I don't like my nose. It's askew from where I connected with the fireplace after refusing the chocolate from father, but it reminds me of what I have endured.

I don't like the wrinkles under my eyes and then I remember that even though I may be on the other side of forty, nearing fifty, each one of those wrinkles reminds me that I have had a great life. I have loved, lost, hugged, cried, travelled, made great friends, lost friends, made stupid mistakes and still I am ok. I don't like that I can't remember stuff without writing it down because of all the drugs that I took, but then I remember how this was my escape - a part of my healing. I don't like my little belly that I've grown during lock down. Then I remember that I got to spend seven months with my incredible family that I only get to see over weekends.

So before degrading, insulting, and ridiculing yourself, look at those little 'imperfections' and remember your story and smile -

You are perfectly imperfect and 100% unapologetic!

More about Robin

Robin, Australian born, African raised and London educated runs her successful fitness business from a rural Victorian town. She grows women to take back their strength through powerlifting, changing their focus, to change their results.

Her unorthodox and abrasive attitude delivers a tough love approach to redesigning her clients lives. Robin believes we are taught to think of our bodies as decorative, as objects to be looked at; powerlifting teaches us to think of our bodies as functional, not passive objects for another's regard. Whole industries exist to profit by removing our confidence and selling it back as external objects. Powerlifting gives back confidence.

Robin has gone from a hippie upbringing, to growing up with family abuse, losing a daughter at 23 and a foray into drugs to drown out life. Realising that destiny was her decision alone, Robin started her journey of recovery. Studying law and then accounting and recently completing MBA, Robin strives to better herself, to better serve those she comes into contact with.

Robin believes a satisfied life is better than a successful life,because our success is measured by others ,but our satisfaction is measured by our own soul, mind and heart

We need to celebrate our stories, our lives are so unique, our screenplays have different plots, twists and cliff hangers. Our theme music is different, characters come and go and the amount of chapters vary.

It's wasteful and naive to compare your chapter 1 to someone else's chapter 6 and to compare your intro to someone else's highlight show reel on social media.

Imagine your life contributing to the library of life and realise that your life forms the fabric of now.

Robin Ross

Strength &Conditioning Coach and Nutritionist

Meet Cheralyn Darcey

There is no Shangri-La out there, no perfect love and light group of souls who are waiting for you to join them. There are humans with all the same dramas, baggage, and annoying qualities that you have but together, you can create and be a part of something that makes a difference to the world and to you.

www.cheralyndarcey.com

https://www.facebook.com/cheralyn.darcey

Finding Me Through Community

Step one: find yourself and then you can be as unapologetic as you please. If you discover what drives you and how you fit into this world, there will be no need for apologies. I know of only one way to do that and that's because in my early 20's I tried a few of them and failed. I've been the hermit, the closeted writer and even the lone sulking creator and while that may work for some, I believe humans are meant to work together. I found 'community' and my heart expanded and there was me, but it took a while.

There is this whole belief, especially in certain circles, that it is the most noble of aspirations to have no need for society. Often found with creatives and especially spiritual people, those who can work in silence, without others around them or being part of anything are the most revered. You are somehow not as good as those who are up there in their hermitage. While it may be just the ticket for those with that inherit personality, it is not in any way better than or higher than those of us who are community creatures. It's not a goal most of us need to aspire to. Being a lone wolf or untouchable hermit who despises society is held in some sort of esteem that I fell for when I was younger and it caused a lot of angst along the way because, well I just lied to myself. I did in fact love being around people. I was fascinated with how others did things, history, culture, travel, and I wanted to learn and read stories about others and listen to what they thought.

My love of art, poetry, of botanical history writings and garden journals exploded when I was in my mid 20's and it triggered in me the need to know more, see more and most importantly for my personal development, be a part of and experience what I was discovering. Could I do it alone? Maybe, but there is such a richness and brightness found when you immerse yourself with others into a field of interest that cannot be felt or drawn upon sitting within the four walls of your tower. You need to get out there and be with others and get your hands dirty, your heart filled, and your mind expanded, in person.

It is uncomfortable if you have told yourself, you don't need others, it is painful if you are in any way self-conscious and it can be annoying and even heart breaking when things go wrong, and they will go wrong. I still find myself being disappointed with people, society, and the world but because I am an active part of the community, and the world is more than one pocket of people I know I can simply move on. Nothing is ever wasted because everything we experience shapes us.

Working in retail, I took with me the empathy to listen to people and really hear what they wanted. Working as a bar tender, I learned that you can never take people at face value or for granted. Being a teacher showed me that we all learn and comprehend in vastly different ways, and it gave me the precious gift of patience. Writing books helped me accept that not everyone is going to like what I do and that's ok. Creating art? Ditto! Having my heat broken showed me what I did not want in the future and what I needed to improve in myself. Being used and abused gave me the strength to stand up and be a fighter not just for myself but also others.

So, how did I find me in all of this? I didn't start with a destination; I began in a direction. People waste way too much time trying to work out what they want to be instead of just stepping into the arena of where they want to be. The 'who' works itself out along the way. This is the advice I gave my children and it's the answer I give to anyone seeking their purpose or their passion. What do you like? What makes you feel good and do not listen to anyone else on this one.

I don't have goals, ever. I have directions and the goals take care of themselves. I'm an author who shares what she loves, an artist that thrives in the atmosphere of creativity and a gardener who loves learning. My goals develop as I learn and experience the direction that I have set myself upon. This means I am never disappointed in failure because I have no defined expectations. Make no mistake, I do not float around without drive and dedication. I am focused on the experience and being part of the whole.

To this end, I am a community gardener, a published botanical history author and artist, a gardening radio presenter and producer and a gardening newspaper columnist. Yes, that's amongst other things but my direction was people and plants. The other stuff just grew along the route of my direction and the best parts? I have found such wonderful friends, a never-ending stream of opportunities to create my own work and I am happy. Incredibly so.

Putting community first and taking my ego out of the equation has led to a life that has grown organically to hold and support me.

The greatest lesson though that I was ever given was not one in where I wanted to be at all. One day I was sitting sipping tea with a well-known author. We were discussing her body of work and how popular it was. I said, "Well, we would do it in some form or another even if it wasn't popular." I was stunned by her answer. She looked me straight in the eyes and said, "I wouldn't, I'd just do something else." I knew that day that I probably wasn't cut out for the field that my work had landed in but her cold words were a gift that made me understand who I was and where I didn't want to be. I was already doing community work and her attitude was polar opposite to the environment that community was all about and to how my heart worked.

Without community work I cannot be me. Without community involvement, I have found in the past that I'm just an island of self, living day to day without any real fulfilment. I really believe that we all need to be connected to something to live a good and happy life and no matter what else we do, having a positive and non-self-serving relationship with our community is vital to internal happiness. "To give without the need to receive" really is a key to immense personal freedom and peace. Something outside of ourselves to anchor us, to focus on, to help us extend ourselves and to even bring us home when need be. Maybe it is called a passion or a purpose but it's not something you find 'out there'; I believe it's just within you. The trick is to discover what makes you. I really don't think this can be done alone. We need to see how our theories about us work and how they might even fail.

Although the hints were always there for me, I never realised the simplicity of what made me tick until later in life. I was busy just doing what I loved and that included teaching, helping at the local schools, community events, environment centres and wherever I landed to be honest. I felt that I was somewhat talented in visual arts, confident in speaking and teaching and that it was up to me, and those like me, to share those skills. I value community, kindness, fairness, truth, and transparency. These are non-negotiables for me, and it all starts with community. Without being an active member for action in my community, I would not be me. I would not have found myself, my real passions, or my true purpose.

So many are looking for a better place to live, new friends, the perfect job, improved relationships but too few realise how easy it is to simply stand up, get their hands dirty and create the environment that will enable these things to materialise. I'm not saying you will get it all, but you will improve your quality of life drastically and opportunity will swing your way much more easily. It all starts with sharing some of what you have without the need to drag out a balance sheet or undervaluing yourself. 'What's in it for me' is so often our first thought, but it shouldn't even be in the equation. 'What's in it for us' is where we need to put our resources and mindset. Once you shift your thinking like this, life changes so much for the better. Will it be perfect? No. Nothing is. Like a rather well-known band once said, while you might not get what you want - "You just might find you get what you need".

You may also think you have nothing to share but after decades of community engagement with groups from Scouts to environmental organisations, museums to community radio and everything in between, I can assure you that there is more of a need for just a warm body to be there. To share my time with others is the greatest gift I have ever had the privilege of giving. My skills as a gardener, artist, speaker, and writer are all of value but equally and sometimes more so are my abilities to stand at a door and direct people, answer phones, listen to a child read a story, to clean a toilet or show somebody how to water a garden. Simple things that just entail showing up.

Because I am so busy and involved in many projects, an outsider perhaps thinks I am talking from a pedestal of privilege, that I have unlimited time, connections, and resources. I don't and at times I've had next to none. All your community asks of you is that you plug in when and how you can, even if that's an hour a week or a few days a month. You give what you can when you can and in the manner you can afford. No one should be asking you to give what you don't have or to force you into personal deficit. Your emotional, mental, and physical needs must be met first, but the secret is this - by giving a bit, you will be filled. If you are reading this and saying, "Oh I used to volunteer at such and such and it drained me, you are wrong Cheralyn" then you need to hear this, you were doing it wrong.

Right now, I work with an incredible group of people at the S.W.A.M.P (Sustainable Wetlands Agricultural Makers Project), a community garden and paddock to plate educational initiative. Our core group is made up of young families, retirees, and those still taking their first steps in life and although everyone has different skills that we joyfully receive, we must also accept that we all also have different commitments and capabilities. This means that there is no expectation that each member will give a set about of time or resources to the project. What is expected is honest dedication and that all members hold space for each other when need be. The freedom of the heart that this gives is immeasurable and it is up to every leader in community projects to make this clear from the start. If you are asking people to forgo their personal lives and needs to create your vision, no matter how beneficial it may be, you are a cult, not a community.

That space I am talking about that we hold for each other at SWAMP is the space to have slow days, no show days, be of no help, to make mistakes and to be ourselves. The others gladly take up the slack because next time it could be them and yes some of us go through longer bouts of being less useful than others but that is where the letting go of the balance sheet thinking comes in. While no community project really benefits from those who are obviously just wasting the time and efforts of the group, just know that these show ponies they usually don't stick around longer than it takes to grab the kudos they are seeking.

Community gardening friends are family. There is no way around it or better description of the relationships you will make should you take the plunge into gardening. They cannot be described in any other way. If you work the earth with a bunch of people, no matter how alike or different they are from you, there is something that grows between you that can't be denied. Then you meet fellow community gardeners from afar and the warmth of knowing and openness between you is similar. I'm a navy wife and mother who has had to uproot my family and travel across the globe at times and the easiest way to find a family vibe and to understand more about where I am is to garden. If you are not a gardener, never fear as there are so many roles in making any botanical initiative run from administration to fund raising and just making sure the gates are opened.

Along my 'plants and people' direction I found my drive to share what I know and while I do this through published titles, I also share my plant and gardening knowledge via Community Radio and Newspapers. 'Down in the Garden' is a weekly gardening page for my local community newspaper that is now syndicated across three other papers and found in a digital edition. I also produce and present a weekly two hour live gardening show, 'At Home with the Gardening gang' on my local community radio station, Coast fm963. What surprises me is that others who are passionate about their work don't do something similar. I am more surprised that I didn't think of it sooner myself and I'm not patting myself on the back here for discovering it as I really did fall into it. After a few years of being interviewed on radio and tv for my work and being told I should give radio a try for myself, I fronted up at my local community radio station to see if they would like a gardening show.

The COVID pandemic had just started in early 2020, and they had a show called 'What's On' every Saturday morning and there was nothing on to report as the state was in lockdown so my gardening show got a trial. What started out as a one-hour fill-in became, 'At Home with the Gardening Gang', a two hour live show that was an awarded finalist in the 2021 Australian Community Broadcasting Awards. Timing was everything I'll agree but I have been surprised while watching others start at the station that is not unusual for those who are willing to do the work. After a few short months, anyone can have the skills to produce, research, present, report and even pick up the technical skills required to pane a radio program. Here's an interesting point for those wanting to expand their audience, there are more people listening to community radio than commercial radio and a whole lot more opportunities for those who want to learn and to share.

After listening to what our gardening show audience appreciated about the program, I was prompted to stay on and to evolve the show into what they needed not what I thought I needed to say or promote about myself. What people wanted was local gardening knowledge true, but what they desired was to feel good, to be uplifted and to laugh. The world had gone crazy, and they were stuck at home so to hear local voices who were just there, who showed up, were dependable, could have a bit of a laugh while providing information they could utilise was greatly appreciated.

A huge lesson I learned quickly in radio was that people are only interested in you for so long, after that you better be talking about them, or you lose them. It is also hard to fake this level of care for others over the radio. People can feel it and they won't stay tuned for long. You need to truly want to be there for the audience, not yourself. The benefits for yourself will come and in spades (sorry!), but only to those who are sharing from a place of truth. Being a part of my community comes first and the rest just grows.

I live by the line 'Passion decides fate' because no matter if your passion is for something positive or negative, it is going to decide where you find yourself, so you better be very careful as to where you focus your passions! If it is just yourself, things are going to get lonely, and your resources drained quickly and often. Community is my heart; I am a community passionate soul who thrives when living and working as a part of the village I find myself in. There is no Shangri-La out there, no perfect love and light group of souls who are waiting for you to join them. There are humans with all the same dramas, baggage, and annoying qualities that you have but together, you can create and be a part of something that makes a difference to the world and to you.

Unapologetically.

More about Cheralyn

Cheralyn Darcey is a gardener with a passion for ethnobotany and botanical history. She produces and presents a live weekly two-hour gardening radio show, 'At Home with the Gardening Gang', on CoastFM 963.

She writes the weekly gardening page 'Down in the Garden', syndicated across four print newspapers and a digital edition.

Cheralyn shares her passion for gardening in her role as the Garden Curator of SWAMP (Sustainable Wetlands Agricultural Makers Project). Based in the middle of the NSW Central Coast, it is a working Community Garden and Urban Farm which provides community outreach programs and community garden training.

She has written and illustrated twenty botanical titles that share with readers her love for plants and lifelong research that explores the relationships of the botanical kingdom and us.

Living on the Central Coast of NSW, Australia, Cheralyn has created and nurtures her own extensive flower, vegetable, native plant and indoor gardens that has been featured in national and international publications and is her creative sanctuary. She is also a Garden Designer, Gardener and Florist who works with the principles of sustainably and creating spaces with deeper personal meaning.

Meet Kerrie Atherton

No matter who we are, where we come from or what we do, at the end of the day when the lights go out and we are all alone, we are all the same. Emotions in skin. We are all human.

www.storiesofhope.com.au

https://www.facebook.com/StoriesofHOPEAustralia

The Girl Who Broke Through: The Face of Alcoholism

A story of an alcoholic.
Her messed up journey of addiction.
Her recovery.
And her ongoing purpose to help people from all walks of life who are struggling through life, find HOPE.

My name is Kerrie and I am an alcoholic

As I sat in a 12-step meeting that night a shaking suicidal wreck of a girl, I never thought I could stay sober for one day let alone the rest of my life. Earlier that day I had planned to end my life. That was 40 years ago and since that day, I have remained sober.

Each of us has a past. Some have suffered more trauma than others. But for us to live a worthwhile life, one must move past the point of being a victim and into that of being a victor. There, a wonderful future awaits. I never chose the path life had for me. I always dreamed of being a famous jazz musician, just like my grandfather and my father. Or an actress on the big stage with all the lights and beautiful costumes to be adored by many for the quirky creative person I was on the inside. But fate had other plans.

For many years, I felt ripped off, but I never knew what great future lay around the corner. At the time, it felt more like a very long and winding road, but in the scheme of life, it was still a corner.

Having said that, I would not change the experiences I had to endure even though they were filled with much trauma, depression, anxiety, and many triggers, to lead to the life I live today. Because of the path my life took, I have been privileged to walk alongside the most broken of broken, the most unloved and judged of society, the rich and famous who appear to have it all on the outside but are just like the rest of us on the inside - emotions in skin with invisible scars. Addiction is no respecter of persons. At the end of the day, we are all just human.

These experiences have gifted me with a rare ability to empathize with those who have suffered on the deepest level. I have been privy to some of the darkest secrets of those who have never dared to bare their soul to another human being. But someone like me, who has walked a similar path and is prepared to share my own experiences gives them a sense of trust and a knowing that I too have suffered and may have some kind of understanding of what they may be going through.

To be able to have come out the other end of the trials I have faced, empowered and full of victory, much stronger in capacity and much richer in spirit than before and to be able to bring HOPE to those on the journey in their darkest moments, gives me joy that's indescribable and something that no amount of money could ever buy. To be able to play a small part in helping change the life of another for good is a gift. To have had the privilege of deep relationships on a heart connection far beyond the menial talk of weather, and to see the beauty in the smallest of things, has enabled me to learn deep gratitude on this journey.

This is my story. Alcoholism didn't win. I am the girl who broke through and one day at a time, thanks to the grace of God, I have not picked up a drink.

"I am an extraordinarily strange girl living in the midst of ordinary circumstances," was what I thought at the time. But looking back now, I was an ordinary and very complex girl living in extraordinarily tumultuous circumstances.

Seeing my father cry for the first time was devastating to me. It was as if a tragedy had happened. It was just an argument. Many of which him and I'd had before. How could I be so awful that I had made my father cry? What I didn't know then was that my father was almost at rock bottom. Watching my mum grapple daily with alcoholism was becoming too much for him to bear. It would have been much easier for him if I just did as I was told. But I was a rebel and even from an early age, no matter how hard I tried to comply, nobody was going to tell me what to do.

The fact that dad would go off to work each morning leaving his depressed wife with us three young children and not knowing how she would cope each day had taken its toll. It wasn't my fault, just another episode in the daily struggle of life that would tip him over the edge. I loved my dad so much and seeing him cry broke my heart.

"Hey Kerrie Anne, what's your game now can anybody play?" A very average but catchy tune that came out in the '60s. My

name is Kerrie Anne, so it had a lasting and comforting effect when my dad would playfully sing it to me. But my life wasn't anything like a game and more like a charade. Never feeling like I fit in, but more like an alien with two heads, preschool was my first real taste of social life on the outside and it was a frightening place.

The truth is that I would have loved to have had many friends to play games with me, but I felt totally alone in the big wide world. My only refuge in those early years was amidst the calm chaos of my home with my family, but particularly time spent with my dad, with whom I'd always had a close connection. We had a lot in common. He had also grown up with an alcoholic mother. I was born on the same day as his father (also an alcoholic). He had been an alcoholic. I was yet to become an alcoholic. He was musical. I was musical. We were creatives. We spoke a silent code. Who would have thought that the words to songs just like *Hey Kerrie Anne* could have such a lasting impact and pierce through a world spiraling out of control to bring moments of such joy and happiness in the midst of turmoil?

It was the tender age of 10 when I first swallowed a mood changing pill. It was anti-anxiety and anti-depressant medication, prescribed for me by a psychiatrist after I'd had a breakdown. A culmination of childhood trauma was the reason. Raised in a home with two alcoholic parents, witnessing my mum being electrocuted and coming back to life when I was seven, being sexually assaulted by a pedophile whilst on holidays at nine years old then to top it all off, I was being bullied at school, was too much trauma for a young girl to cope with. After we returned from the holiday from hell, I lived constantly swallowed by fear. I was convinced the attacker knew where we lived because when we had checked in for our holiday, we had to give our address. We later found out by the police, that he was the son of the owner of the holiday cabins. From that day I lived in terror that he would find me. It would not be until I was 25 years old before I would open my bedroom window again at night.

It's no doubt I broke down at ten years old. Pills became my crutch to get me through life and I became addicted.

For a while, they took the edge off fear, insecurity and pain and I felt a pulling towards their effects more and more. They were a way to escape the harshness of my reality. But they didn't do enough. The fear I was experiencing was becoming crippling along with the public humiliation I felt at school. Wherever I went out in public for that fact. The internal dialogue I believed about myself from a young age was that 'I was deficit and that something was very wrong with me'. The outside world was a very frightening place and I felt like a raw exposed nerve.

At 15 I discovered alcohol. After having my first drink of a cask of boiling hot wine that had been hidden under our neighbour's caravan across the road, I felt violently sick, but on the inside of my mind I felt as though a light had switched on. Everything felt like sunshine, and the black cloud that had always hung over my head went missing into the abyss. I felt like alcohol coloured me in. I told myself, 'I have just found the very thing that will truly help me get through life'. From that very first drink though something was wrong. I couldn't stop at one. It was as if, one was too many, and 100 was not enough. Within weeks my newfound life was spinning out of control and quickly.

I had been attending Alateen meetings and one night soon after I met a boy. His father was also an alcoholic. We were both there trying to seek support to deal with the damage alcohol had done to our family units. This relationship would turn out to be the perfect storm. He became my first boyfriend. He was 17. It was only a matter of a few months before he was pleading with me not to drink anymore when he took me out on dates and I couldn't understand why.

I was 16 when I first entered the 12 step rooms of recovery but only for a look. I was not ready to stop. The 12 traditions of this program say that we are not allowed to say the name of this fellowship in media or print but I'm sure everyone out there knows exactly which fellowship I am talking about. Let's just say the round circle that you see on American movies where a person says, 'my names John and I'm an alcoholic', that one.

Over here in Australia it's not always a circle and more like a theatre style setting only the stories we are listening to and sharing about as is in any meeting around the world, are not love stories, or comedies, but heart wrenching, death defying, gruelling accounts of suffering at the hands of what was once our best friend, alcohol and substances.

There comes a point in every addict or alcoholic's life where this best friend eventually turns its back on each and every one of us and leaves us fighting desperately for our very existence. This is the point of rock bottom. Some people say they have a few rock bottoms, and I had a few. Everyone's rock bottom looks different. But the ultimate rock bottom is the one that eventually rips everything out of you, leaves you totally naked, bare and hopeless, and leaves you with nothing except a deep knowing inside your soul, that in order to live, things must change. My rock bottom was coming soon.

In those rooms, everybody smoked except me. It was the lesser of the evil addictions and usually the last addiction to be broken. I thought I was going to suffocate sitting there having a look in those smoke-filled rooms, but there was something else I was also breathing in which kept me pinned to my seat as I intently listened, my eyes glued to those speakers, and It was 'LIFE mixed with fear and HOPE'.

Even in the midst of my emptiness, even breathing in life, finding life, looking through a distant lens at life in all its mess and what it could be, listening to the ones still going through it and the stories of hope of the ones who had come out the other side of addiction, wasn't enough to keep me there for long and something I had certainly not counted on, was the fear that gripped me as I heard the horror stories of what waited for me if I kept drinking. Those stories pierced me to the core and never left my thoughts. They lingered like the voice of a bad best friend, plaguing me with a sense of reason and a warning that if I kept drinking, those things could happen to me. I kept pushing them back to the farthest part of my mind.

I didn't want to hear those stories; I was way too young to end up like those people. They were way sicker than I, was what I thought. Yet in the midst of my distorted ego and emotional immaturity, I had devised a plan. I was only going there for a few quick visits, not once, twice but a handful of times for the sole reason to get my parents and boyfriend who kept insisting 'I was an alcoholic', or at very least, kept trying to tell me I had a serious problem with my drinking, off my back.

Much to my surprise, when I first laid eyes on the walls in the 12 step rooms there were many slogans and sayings plastered all over making them look like a big collage. There were also many mantras spoken by the older wiser members, and the one that never left me, that taunted me every time I drank, the one that greeted me and my thoughts at the dawn of every hangover was 'If you're an alcoholic and continue to come to these rooms and don't get the program, THE PROGRAM WILL GET YOU.

I was scared!

Who wants to be an alcoholic at 16? No one. 'It's not possible' I thought. My life wasn't over like all those people sitting in those rooms who were pointing at me as they spoke saying things like, 'I wish I had found this program when I was your age, then I wouldn't have lost my family, my home, ended up in a mental ward, ended up in jail, lost my license, killed someone, lost my kids, lost my health, lost my career, basically losing EVERYTHING.

But as every sixteen-year-old must do, I got on with my life. On with my drinking and at the same time simultaneously on with trying to prove to every single person that spoke against my ability to control my drinking, the fact that, 'I was not an alcoholic'. What the naysayers didn't know was that I had made a secret deal with myself like an insurance - assurance policy that if I ever got as bad as them, those sick people in those rooms, I knew where to go. Back to the place of no return.

Nevertheless, first I had some more hard core proving to do to convince everyone I was in control, so I made an announcement, 'I was giving up drinking for three months.' Surely, I could not be an alcoholic if I could do that. It had been a very long three months. Feeling proud of myself, and at an all-time high, I decided I deserved a celebration. How does any alcoholic celebrate? With a drink of course. Not just one, but two, three, four ,and I can't remember what happened next but that night as with many nights to come, I ended up paralytic. Just like the months prior. Nothing had changed.

What I still didn't get was the fact 'that it was the first drink that does the damage'. That once I had one, I couldn't stop. So not drinking for three months at that stage seemed relatively easy but now we were back to square one and I still didn't think I had a problem. In true alcoholic form, I played the blame game, blaming everything around me. Everything except alcohol.

I hated school, I was very insecure around my boyfriend, my relationship was fractured with my parents. My mum had only become sober three years prior, and my dad was a sober recovering alcoholic. Both my parents though very loving had extremely short fuses and would go off like firecrackers. My brothers were close and had each other, I felt all alone. I had every reason to drink.

Very quickly things started declining. My boyfriend was putting pressure on me to have sex, something I hadn't done before. I felt very triggered afraid and disgusted especially after the trauma of the sexual assault when I was nine. It was the last thing I wanted to do, but as many young girls believe, I thought if I didn't give in to his constant demands and do the deed, my boyfriend would leave me. If he left me, I thought my life would be over. I already thought I was unlovable, and I needed him like the air I breathed.

I felt like I had no choice. So, one afternoon after being at an Alateen meeting together, I had my first consensual experience, if you can even call it that, on the cold hard cement floor of the toilet block at the primary school premises where we met for the meetings. Our relationship had now taken on a new meaning, and I had never felt more insecure!

As crazy as it sounds, I was going to Alateen to learn how to survive in a family with alcoholic parents, but I was drinking at the same time, and abusing pills on a daily basis. I was also sexually active. I felt disgusting. Like a bad girl. My whole demeanour changed and the F*** word became a constant part of my vocabulary. I was angry with the world. I was angry with myself. My self-esteem had never been lower. I hated myself. I had no friends. I was so lonely. Many years of bullying and public humiliation had festered inside me, and I couldn't hold in the pain any longer. It was time to unleash myself. I exploded.

My drinking escalated and so did my aggression. I became a violent drunk and things like attacking my boyfriend, smashing my fist on his windscreen, running off into the night in a frenzy to end up who knows where became regular occurrences. Only afterwards to be filled with so much shame and regret for my actions while drunk was almost unbearable. The only thing that would fix what I felt inside was to have another drink to blot out all the pain. And on went the cycle of addiction. Eventually our relationship ended after fifteen months. I felt abandoned, like my soul had been ripped out and didn't know how I could go on another day. I had been suicidal prior to that and would often smash my head into my bedroom wall because I hated myself so much. Now these thoughts were plaguing me on a daily basis. I dreaded waking up and I didn't know how to live.

There are many things that still remain a mystery about my drinking days and forty years on, I still have flashbacks of things, people and places like a bad disjointed movie that makes no sense. Like a jigsaw puzzle that has no end.

My life just kept playing out like a bad movie and I fell into the next relationship which ended up being even more damaging. Something very bad happened to me in this relationship and I have lived with the consequences my whole life since. Up to this point I was still what we call a functioning alcoholic. I still held down my job as a receptionist and drank most nights after work hiding bottles under my bed. But soon my job would be affected by my drinking. I started having days off, having blackouts, not remembering what happened on weekends. I started trying other drugs and then one terrible weekend my life almost ended when I accidently overdosed on a mixture of pills, weed and alcohol. I had collapsed on the floor of the nightclub toilets and was watching my lifeless body as I hovered above it, begging God to let me live. I did a deal with him that night. If he let me live, I would come clean and tell my parents the true extent of my addiction and how out of control my life was. I kept up my end of the bargain. But it was no surprise to them as they watched on helplessly as the daughter they loved so much was slowly destroying her life before their very eyes. 'But I knew where to go if I got that bad' and I was getting closer each passing day.

It's very hard to describe the emotional pain and desperation an addicted person goes through on a daily basis. I was emotionally, physically, and spiritually bankrupt. I felt so alone, hopeless, ashamed and sick. I knew I was walking on a knife's edge but I couldn't stop drinking. I was terrified of falling off the edge, but I literally didn't know how I could let go of alcohol.

Then at seventeen, one fateful night while drunk I was raped. I never told a soul. I thought there would be no justice, so I slowly started shrinking inside with shame and drank even more to try and escape from the pain of shame. But still it wasn't enough to stop me, and I kept on going. Another relationship, this time more violent than the previous relationships. Toxic to the core. Another alcoholic. It would only take three short months for the day to come. Things were now that bad. It was the day after I came home from a holiday with my violent boyfriend. He had punched me in front of families in the waiting room at the caravan park. I couldn't take any more.

Even though I had always held the original plan in my head of what I would do if my life got that bad, I woke up on this day totally devoid of all hope. I formulated another plan, and that was to end my life. It was January 17, 1982.   This would be the day when I would put an end to all the internal suffering. I didn't want to die, but I just didn't know how to live anymore. Just at that moment, I heard a loud voice which I believe was the voice of God, say 'Don't do it! If you hold on a bit longer, you will find happiness one day.' True happiness is all I had ever longed for. I'd had many happy times in my life but those days or moments, were always marred by a black cloud hanging over my head. That black cloud was depression.

At the most crucial point in my life, God's plan and my plan would collide. After hearing his voice, I knew I had one chance left. My original plan. I went back to a meeting that night and miraculously, I have never had a drink since that day. I truly am a walking miracle who can now offer great HOPE to anyone out there battling trauma and addictions of any kind.

If I could get off, you too can get off the merry go round.

When an alcoholic or addict starts abusing a substance, their emotional growth stops there. Therefore, when I put down alcohol and pills, my emotional maturity was that of a ten-year-old. I cried every day for around two years. I couldn't handle criticism, conflict, anger, jealousy or fear. It took me many years to work through and learn how to navigate these emotions in a healthy way.

As life is, it has been a rollercoaster over my forty years in recovery. There have been many highs and many lows. I have had to do life on life's terms with no inebriation from the cold harshness of life. But I have had the opportunity to truly experience every emotion to its fullest. From exhilaration and excitement to joy and sadness, anger, and fear. Every single experience has taught me a lot about resilience and a lot about the absolute beauty of life.

The day I stopped drinking, I entered an abusive relationship and stayed trapped in it for three years. But I stayed sober. I suffered severe post-natal depression after the birth of both my children, but I stayed sober. I lost a baby to miscarriage, but I stayed sober. I suffered extensive grief and guilt when my hubby I and our two children moved interstate and left my extended family in Sydney. Only to find out a year and a half later that my mum had cancer. She only lasted four years. The grief was unbearable, but I stayed sober. Then my dear dad who I was so close to passed away after a long illness, but I didn't pick up a drink. I have experienced many hard times over the years, and I mention these difficult times so you the reader will know that resilience, sobriety and joy in the midst of hard times is possible and that at the end of every storm the light will appear again.

If I had picked up a drink through these hard times, all alcohol would have ever done for me would be take away the pain temporarily, but I would still have to face the emotional pain and reality of life's difficulties after its effects were over. I would have too much to lose.

Through the years, I have experienced depression but having learned how to put strategies in place to help me stay sober I am able to manage my emotions well these days. As a result of my nature, environment, early childhood trauma and my upbringing which gave me an unrelenting resolve not to conform or blur my morals or boundaries just to fit into this world to be popular, I have often been left out, isolated, lonely, judged, and misunderstood, but I haven't picked up a drink. I have always felt different, and I am okay with being different. I celebrate my unique qualities today. Today, I colour myself in. I am not defined by my past it has merely shaped me and shaped me greatly into someone who deeply cares for others. One of my greatest desires is that nobody in this world would ever feel like they have to do life alone. Having had great difficulty with friendships growing up, I heard a great saying in sobriety, 'if you want to have a friend, you have to be a friend'. Once I learned to get past my own self centeredness, I was able to concentrate on the needs of others. Consequently, I have so many meaningful relationships and great friendships today.

Something I have learned is that if you can help change one person's life, you just don't know what a world-changer that one person is going to go on to be.

I have written several programs and key notes where I have shared the experiences of my life and my resiliency and determination for survival. These have been presented on various stages and also in schools which have helped change the lives of many students. If someone had intervened in my life, maybe it would have turned out very differently. But there was no intervention. Because of this, I have stood in the gap for all the hurting young people out there who felt they had no one.

Because I had seen the most broken of broken and walked alongside those whom society rejects, I desired for everyone to feel accepted and loved. My husband and I founded a program for the homeless and disadvantaged on the Sunshine Coast called Streetlight. This organisation showed people that they were valuable and loved, despite where they found themselves in life. Many said that because of the acceptance we showed them without judgement, and our ability to love them right where they were at, it helped to transform their lives. After all, we are not defined by our past and all on a journey.

In January 2017, after experiencing a long period of grief from the loss of both of my parents and watching my husband battle with illness and burnout, I came to a point where I felt utterly defeated. This was another rock bottom. I knew this feeling from before, but this time it felt worse than ever, and I really felt like picking up a drink. I barely felt like I could go on. All Hope seemed lost. I felt very alone. Having become the person others went to for refuge and help, I found myself in a dark tunnel barely able to see the light. I have heard the comment all too often, "Kerrie, you look like you have it all together." Well, I want to tell the world right now, everyone needs encouragement. Never presume someone is just okay. Often, it's the people you would least expect who can be suffering internally the most.

After a couple of months of isolating myself from the outside world and spending much of my time alone in deep reflection with one whom I did find solace in - God - slowly the pain started to heal and I didn't pick up a drink. Knowing I needed connection I forced myself to attend a women's conference. There was a defining moment that day as I saw three people up on stage. These people were sharing their stories of how they had overcome adversity and found a purpose to go on.

I started thinking about all the things I had been through and the many things I had overcome in my life and realised that if these brave people could stand up on that stage after all they have been through and go on to live their life with purpose, I could also. Right there in that room, something powerful happened inside me. I had the 'lightbulb moment' and I was determined that I would not lie down any longer, but I would rise-up. That my pain would not be in vain, and I would use it for others gain. I had the revelation that I had not been through the pain in my life for nothing. I was given the inspiration that day to go on and to inspire and bring HOPE to the multitudes.

Seeing the need so great in our world with lack of human connection at its all-time highest, along with a climbing suicide rate, I thought about all the hard times I had come out of and the many people I also knew who had also overcome such adversity in their lives. I knew that if I could create a space where people could come together from all walks of life, no matter what they believed in or what state they were in, I could literally help change thousands of lives at once.

Three months later, in January 2017, I started Stories of HOPE Australia hosting monthly local events which have continued to this day. With so many needing support and only so many hours in the day, I wanted to start something that could literally reach the masses. Stories of HOPE carries a no religious, political or business agenda policy, because I didn't want any barriers at all. Even though I have my own spiritual beliefs, I hold this all-inclusive policy so the only agenda ever allowed is simply to give and receive HOPE. For such a time as this, the walls come down and genuine connection takes place. People feel accepted and are gathered together for the common good as well as for one another.

At the height of covid in 2021 just after my second book was released, the world went into lockdown. Humanity was screaming for connection and hope like never before. With that in mind, I started an online platform 'Stories of HOPE Worldwide' where I have conversations and continue to interview inspiring humans from all around the world who have come out the other side of hard times. There is no one greater to bring hope and a sense of connectedness to the person still suffering than the one who has walked the journey of lived experience. We are living in a different world now. Helping people to navigate their mental health is of utmost importance to me as I know what it's like to suffer. In addition to my other work as a speaker, counsellor and author, I am now a 'Mental Health First Aid' training instructor. Because I chose sobriety, today the rewards in my story are many. I have an amazing life of meaning and purpose. I have been married for thirty-four years. I have two amazing children and an amazing son and daughter in law. I have two adorable granddaughters. I live in one of the most beautiful places in the world where I can look at the beach every single day. I have wonderful relationships. I feel truly blessed. It could have nearly been a very different story had I ended my life that day.

As has been the case for me in the 12 step rooms, there comes a time in everyone's life when they will need to hear a story of HOPE. That story could be the very thing that goes on to show us our purpose, to cause us to know that we are not alone in our struggles and that there are others who have gone before us and have come out the other side stronger than ever before.

Hearing a story of HOPE can be a lifeline to hold on to. People need to know that their life is worth living. That they were born for a greater purpose. Today is the first day of the rest of your life and despite what has been, the rest of your life can be much greater than the past. Grace means that we all deserve a second chance. We all need HOPE. Connection is vital for the human soul to flourish. Ultimately faith, HOPE and love are the things that have the greatest power to change lives. Faith and HOPE for a greater tomorrow and love for one another.

'No matter who we are, where we come from or what we do, at the end of the day when the lights go out and we are all alone, we are all the same. Emotions in skin. We are all human'. 'You are never too young or too old to make a difference in this world, and never too old to achieve your dreams. I found my greatest purpose at fifty-three and I feel like I am just getting started. Live your life unashamed. Be kind. Have compassion for yourself and embrace your uniqueness. Don't shrink. Don't stay in the dark. Shine bright. You have been given a special set of gifts and talents and the world needs what you have to offer. Don't do life alone, together is better. Never give up and always hold onto HOPE.

More about Kerrie

Kerrie Atherton Founder of Stories of HOPE Australia/WORLDWIDE and EMPOWER Life Solutions is a Keynote Speaker, Author, Event Host, Trauma and Addictions Recovery Coach/Counsellor and School Program Presenter.

After planning suicide at 18, Kerrie walked through the doors of the 12 Step Room of Recovery Program and since that day 40 years ago, has remained clean and sober. Over the past 30 years, Kerrie has worked in the business and community sector helping those who are struggling with the issues of life find Hope. Since moving to the Sunshine Coast 16 years ago she has worked in a voluntary capacity in the community as well as private practice as a trauma and addictions coach/counsellor and mentor building connection and supporting people from all walks of life. In addition, she has worked with many young people in crisis at different schools on the Sunshine Coast.

Along with her husband she founded a charity called "Streetlight" which ran for six years supporting the homeless and disadvantaged. Four years ago, Kerrie founded "Stories of HOPE Australia" a platform which runs monthly events bringing HOPE to the community and is now a published author having just released the second book in her, "Stories of HOPE Australia" series 'Resilient People, Remarkable Stories'.

When the world went into lockdown, Kerrie commenced Stories of HOPE WORLDWIDE an online platform sharing stories of HOPE around the world. Kerrie has also recently become a Mental Health First Aid trainer, helping people to recognise the signs that someone may be experiencing a mental health crisis and how to assist them.

In everything she does, her passion is to help prevent suicide and hopelessness and to bring HOPE to people in times of uncertainty in a rapidly changing world.

Meet Michelle Worthington

The clarity came on the drive back home. On my own, I was a better person. I could be someone my children could grow to respect. I could teach them how to respect themselves and others. I could show them the true meaning of life and love. But before I did all those things, I had to start respecting and loving myself. I needed to stop looking for miracles and realise I was the miracle.

https://www.linkedin.com/in/michelleworthingtonauthor/

www.michelleworthington.com

The Day That Changed My Life

The day that changed my life started the night before. I had found myself in a slippery place. Pride had wounded me, love had hurt me, sleep had departed from me and I was bringing up a baby a toddler by myself. I couldn't bear to discuss my failed marriage with anyone, but I kept going over and over in my mind where I went wrong. My father knew enough to be shocked into silence and my mother knew I wasn't sleeping, and they both loved me enough not to ask too many questions and help with the boys when they could.

The alarm clock said two am and I was still tossing and turning. I needed to get some sleep. My head hurt as much as my heart. It was exactly one year after I had left my husband that day, I had filed for divorce. Maybe I had my one chance at happiness and I blew it. Maybe he was right, and we should have stayed together for the sake of the children.

A groan broke the silence of the dark. My eldest son was turning in his sleep in the next room. In agony, I got up and sat on the edge of my bed, trying to make sense of the mess inside my head. If I went back to a marriage where I was not valued or respected, my children would have a mother and father who lived under the same roof and loved them very much but didn't love each other. What sort of message was that sending them?

In the morning, I dropped the kids at day-care and drove to visit the grave of my grandfather. I had bought a handkerchief to clean the leaves and dirt from the plaque so that it looked well cared for, as he had done at the grave of his mother. He had always considered it an important task, letting any passers-by know that the person who lay there was as loved in death as they were in life, and never forgotten.

Of course, the handkerchief had other uses. I hadn't cried so hard in a long time. I got down on my knees and asked him to help me. Send me a sign that my life would change for the better. There weren't any voices, or visions or miracles of any kind. Just a tired, heartbroken woman crying over the grave of the one of the most influential people in her life who loved her without judgement, without condition and without holding anything back.

The clarity came on the drive back home. On my own, I was a better person. I could be someone my children could grow to respect. I could teach them how to respect themselves and others. I could show them the true meaning of life and love. But before I did all those things, I had to start respecting and loving myself. I needed to stop looking for miracles and realise I was the miracle.

When I was growing up, I wanted to be a teacher. Being mercilessly bullied at school as a child for being pint-sized and smart, you would hardly think that coming back to school to work for the rest of my life would be a goal. In fact, after the bullying continued in high school, it did become the furthest thing from my mind and I gave up on my dream. When I was at school, I learnt to hide how smart I was, so I didn't get beaten up on the way home or lose my friends who thought I was showing off. I just couldn't figure out the purpose of being smart if it didn't help me or anyone else.

When I got home, I pulled out my old diaries, notebooks and scribble pads that I had written poems and stories on from when I could hold a pen. Stories were my passion. Sharing my stories with the world had always been a goal of mine, until life got in the way. I had nothing left to lose. Opening my diary, a photo fell out. It was a picture of my grandfather, just as I remember him when I was growing up, in his favourite faded football jersey, proudly holding a fish that he had just caught. It was the sign I had been looking for, and I will never forget the day I started writing again. It was the day that changed my life forever.

It is in following our passion that invariably with a sense of relief that we begin to feel like ourselves again. The world has no exclusiveness. It contains everything, provides for everything, welcomes the high and the low, the good and the bad. We human beings are not so broadminded. We discriminate, we approve and disapprove. I decided to become unconditionally grateful for all that I had in my life. Gratitude is not just a feeling anymore; it became my way of life. I had so much to be thankful for. Consciously releasing any feelings of selfishness, envy or resentment, I came to the realisation that what I already had was enough to make me happy. Anything more was a blessing.

Gratitude is not positivity. Positivity is looking for the good in every situation. Gratitude is acknowledging the good and the bad, then choosing a mindset that focuses on a grounding in reality with tangible and existing assets. I used to avoid confrontation at all costs and try to ignore the bad stuff. It needed to be dealt with for it to get out of my way.

I like order and structure and don't feel comfortable with chaos, which had now become the regular atmosphere in our home. I am always looking to connect the dots in our day-to-day randomness in order to identify old patterns of behaviour that are limiting my success in business and am consciously choosing every day to live my best possible life. All the dots kept showing me I needed to do more with my writing. When I finally decided to transition from someone who loved writing to a becoming a published author, I found it was a very easy thing for the people in my life to complacently offer their advice about my new career choice, even recommending it remain a hobby because it didn't fit into the right tax bracket. Nobody should feel the need to hide who they are, or dull their sparkle to fit in, or avoid amazing opportunities to use their talents because of fear of judgement or other people's perceptions.

Most of us are living at a low level of happiness. I had spent years trying to be happy. I did my best in everything I did. I threw myself into supporting my children financially and emotionally. I repressed any selfish feelings. The only way I can describe it was it felt like I was suffering from chronic asthma. There was plenty of air for me to breathe, but there was some sort of obstruction and air couldn't get into my lungs. I didn't need more air; I needed to remove the obstruction. After I had got over the pain and heartbreak of my divorce, I found that I had a new life, a new power and a strength within me that could see me through whatever life threw at me. It was time to start writing again.

Coming from a place of gratitude helped me to find my work deeply rewarding and fulfilling in ways that I didn't in my non-creative-actually-making-money employment. Gratitude allowed me to see more to success than financial gain. Wealth and creativity don't need to be at odds with each other.

At the core of it all, I really wanted to help people. I love people seeing their dreams come true. I love when people discover that they were so much more than what they ever thought they could or would be. I'm passionate about sharing my love of words with the next generation of readers and storytellers. I love talking about engaging special needs kids through sensory storytelling, writing and publishing picture books that all children can see their reflections in and encouraging new voices in children's writing. My vision for the world is for all children to have access to books that they can see their own lives mirrored in and introduce them to the endless possibilities that are theirs for the taking.

At the heart of the problem in making money from doing what I loved was an attitude towards money that I had always struggled with. I had to take a long, hard look at my attitude towards success before dismissing my passion for writing for children as never being profitable. It was easy to feel disheartened when my financial matters felt opposed to my creative efforts.

Too many aspiring authors attempt to put barriers around their creative business, but end up putting them in their own way instead, expecting money to flow in dependable ways through predictable channels. Marketing a creative business is different to a traditional business. Whenever and wherever possible, it needs to have the wriggle room to bend and flex with not only trends in the market, but the ups and downs of creative life.

I decided to align my creative business with what was actually possible using the assets I had available to me at that time, and be flexible enough to change my goals and brand as my career started to grow. It wasn't just my writing that got better, or my bank balance; I did, too.

An aspiring author needs to learn to distinguish glitter from gold. The highly competitive nature of creative businesses means that you will need to work hard to make a living, but this doesn't mean that spectacular success is out of reach. The journey is all part of the fun. I wish I had maybe enjoyed the struggle, which is strange, but it was a huge part of me becoming the unapologetic person I am today.

Fears, doubts and insecurities are part of human nature, but so is being brave enough to follow your passion and embrace your true purpose. For me, doing the hard work required to follow my passion was worth more to me than living a life of unfulfilled potential. Constant spot-fire-fighting, waking up and going to bed in chaos and lack of support can make you feel like there really is no way you could realistically even be a published author. I asked myself "Do I really have what it takes?" Changing my mindset about who I was and what I was capable of was integral in the pathway to my success.

Achieving a work-life balance, providing for my family and setting a good example for my kids is above other things part of what it means to me to be successful. Balancing having the time and energy to look after my family and the time and energy to put into my passion is my top reason for wanting to achieve a work-life balance. When your goal is hard, and your dream is bigger than your comfort zone, can living a dream for someone else really be enough to keep you motivated? Is it so awful to want to achieve something just for yourself? Have we become so scared of being labelled 'selfish' and a 'bad mother' because we want to pursue a career that the term Work-Life Balance is something that is used when we are 'failing' to put our family first? My kids love me and they want me to be happy. But, do they want the dream I have? Do they share my passion? The answer is no. Doing it for them is not enough. I have to do it for the love of writing and working for myself. What other people thought of me was a huge achievement-blocker that needed to be overcome because when my goal became difficult to reach, it would have been very easy to stop and justify failure by saying it didn't turn out to be the right thing for my family, that I didn't have a work-life balance and I could have just listened to the million reasons that circulated constantly in the back of my mind as to why I shouldn't keep trying. What if it was the right thing for me and I just gave in because it meant my family would have had to make some changes and sacrifices for me to achieve it? That is part of achieving a work-life balance, placing your passion as a priority and not always the other way around.

I was the boss. And that meant there was no one standing over my shoulder, telling me what to do next. There is no corporate ladder. No job descriptions. No salaries. No promotions.

Being a creative entrepreneur means wading through murky waters and figuring out your own path to success. This can be extremely daunting, especially when it's your dream to make a living from your writing.

A roadmap could have taken the stress out of exploring new pathways, but I didn't really get one. Some days I had no idea if what I was doing was right. I wasted time comparing myself to other authors. I was living with the feeling of being "not enough",

When I felt like running away from that feeling, that's when I leaned into it instead and learned to embrace that stress. Coffee helped.

I found this analogy interesting and often asked myself these questions on the tough days. I imagined I was holding a cup of coffee when someone came along and bumped into me, making me spill my coffee everywhere.

Why did I spill the coffee? Was it because someone bumped into me? Or did I spill the coffee because there was coffee in my cup? Had it been night time, there would have been tea in the cup and I would have spilled tea. Whatever was inside the cup, is what would spill out.

Therefore, when life came along and bumped me, which happened a lot, whatever was inside me would come out. It's easy to fake it, until you get rattled. When life gets tough, what spills over? Joy, gratefulness, peace and humility? Or anger, bitterness, harsh words and reactions?

It took time to sit quietly with myself in that feeling of discomfort, knowing that I have the courage to pursue my dreams. Because not everyone does. I could be the one in a million. In order to achieve that, my life became a series of attempts to try and do better. Be better.

When I did achieve balance, true balance, it came with the love and support of my family and a business that allows me to give them the time they need along with a mother who is energised and successful with her chosen career. Work-life balance was something I had done for myself as well as my family and I will always be proud of that.

If my story has resonated with you in any way, know that you are not alone. You never have been. You know more now than you have ever known, and yet may be convinced that you know nothing of what you most wish to know. You may distrust more utterly than you have ever mistrusted yourself before, but deep down you know what direction to take and what decisions to make. Your convictions may have suffered a sea-change and are fast melting, if not completely evaporated but the vision stays clear. There is no crystal ball that will allow me to tell you what lies ahead. I am still on the journey and the times to come make no promise of being more settled or more comfortable. We are children, gazing through toy telescopes at the glittering heavens, feeling small and insignificant. We are authors.

Endless possibilities are yours if you will open your eyes and see them. It is time to awake to your possibility. If you do not, and choose to stay asleep when you ought to be awake, to dream when you ought to be doing, you will miss opportunities and be caught in dangers that need a special wakefulness and watchfulness to guard against. Wake up! This could be the day that changes your life.

More about Michelle

Michelle is an international award-winning children's author, scriptwriter and actress. A full-time writer based in Brisbane, Michelle credits her three sons for giving her an endless source of inspiration, as well as her wrinkles.

Two-time winner of the International Book Award, Michelle has twice been short listed for a CBCA Picture Book of the Year Award and Australian Speech Pathology Award. Michelle was the recipient of the 2018 AusMumpreneur Gold Award for Business Excellence and the winner of the 2018 Redlands BaR award for Best Start Up Business.

Her television series scripts have been finalists at international film festivals and her feature film script, Dad's Don't Dance was the winner of the feature film script writing award at the AFIN international film festival.

She has appeared as an extra in both feature films and television series. Michelle is dedicated to encouraging a strong love of reading and writing in young children and enjoys working with charities that support the vision of empowering youth through education.

As a mentor and editor, she helps aspiring authors find pathways to publication and enjoys working as part of a team in projects that are purposeful, innovative, and inspirational.

Meet Nana Mulundiki

If you prick my finger and you prick a white person's we're both going to bleed the same colour of blood; red. That makes us human. That makes us all the same.

https://www.facebook.com/nana.mulundika

https://www.linkedin.com/in/nana-mulundika-2aba06200/

The Journey Of A Lioness

A lot of things come to mind when I think of *Unapologetically Me*. I think of me, the person being free to live a life that I choose and living it proudly and authentically. This hasn't been an easy thing to do. To get to a point of living a fulfilling life unapologetically requires looking at a few things.

Firstly, who was I then? I grew up in Zambia, Africa and in my childhood, I was extremely introverted. I was one of those children and even teens who just loved to observe her surroundings, listening to what was going on around me. I wouldn't say much. I'm not tall (barely reaching 5 foot in heels) and I looked young for my age. Because of being a quiet person, I was quite often misunderstood; thought to be unfriendly and maybe even anti-social. I really loved my own company and spending time reading and not doing things kids my age did.

I now realise It takes a special kind of person to know who they are, what they want out of life, going after it and making no apologies for it. Growing up in Southern Africa was and will always be something I'm immensely proud of and I wouldn't trade it for anything, but it didn't come without its challenges. In those days, the majority of African women were just beginning to realise who they were and the contributions they could make to society and beyond. In a huge number of sectors and industries, women were starting to become powerful contenders and I can vividly remember how thrilling that was. Still, we did hold on to upbringings which meant in a lot of instances women were seen and not heard and made to feel their place was in the kitchen and bedroom.

Growing up, I was never tall enough, not pretty enough and had that said to my face more times than I can remember. I was told I'm both too quiet and too loud. When I'd speak my truth, I was told I was too opinionated and should just sit down. I never fitted in at all. For me, I can recall being taught to have an opinion but not express it, especially if it was contrary to everyone else or wasn't a popular one. And for a very long time that's exactly what I did. I never let anyone know the real me; how could I when I didn't know who I was myself? I found it very easy to just be quiet, never offer anything to the table; as an introvert this was easy, and I did this for many years.

Secondly, I learned very quickly to put up a front. Smile when I was hurting inside and keep to myself pretty much. All the while, the real Nana was suffocating and disappearing. I thought moving to another country would help me rediscover me - what I'm supposed to do with my life. At first that didn't work at all. For example, I always wore my hair natural or in braids. I got offered a job interview for a media company who had seen my pictures but at the interview said that even though I was well qualified, I couldn't go on TV with braided or natural hair. Could I straighten it to look more European? I refused to do so because my natural look was something I loved even if no one else did. I must credit my upbringing and my parents because they did bring me up to believe I could accomplish anything and be whatever I wanted. They gave a good foundation of teaching me to love and appreciate myself and making me believe I was the most beautiful girl no matter what I looked like, and I went through many phases with my looks. I see now that if I was taught to believe I look good with natural hair or straight hair then I probably would have gone along with the request and most definitely would have been unauthentic and miserable.

Needless to say, I never got the job. That was the tipping point for me and is what made me take the journey to rediscover me.

Who then, is the real me? To become authentically me and be unapologetic about it, I had to ask myself a lot of hard questions. I did a lot of reading on the subject and read something that changed me forever. I first asked myself, what is it that is stopping me from living a fulfilling and happy life? A lot of reasons came up with three being the most popular. I've spoken to a lot of people who have indicated the following as well. I realised that I put everyone and everything in my life first. Friends and family's need were always more important than my own. If a friend or family member asked for my help, I would be there even if it meant risking my own physical, mental and emotion help. It was hard to be honest and say NO and this cost me my health and my sanity.

Which brings me to the second reason. Boundaries. I never had them. At all. I was scared to express my boundaries because I thought that people would not respect me or would have a problem with me or would not even love me. This made me a recluse for a while. I realised this after reading posts from a Facebook group and I chuckled because how could I have been so naïve. I didn't know or value my worth. It didn't matter that I was educated or got compliments for my appearance or had true sister friends tell me how worthy I was; I couldn't see it.

This helped me immensely especially when I encountered racism. That was the first time I was made to feel that I am not worthy simply because of the colour of my skin. I was made to feel that I was not educated enough simply because of the colour of my skin. I was made to feel that black is not beautiful; that black cannot function. That black people cannot contribute to society and that black people cannot do so many things. This weighed down on me for quite a long time messing with my self-esteem, messing with my emotions and I had to take a moment to ask myself why would I want to listen to somebody that doesn't know anything about me? Why would I want to listen to anybody who doesn't know anything about what it's like to be a black woman? Why would I listen to anybody who doesn't know anything about what it's like to live in a foreign country? Anything about what it's like to look different but still be the same.

I'm sure you've all heard of this cliche - We are still the same. If you prick my finger and you prick a white person's finger, we're both going to bleed the same colour of blood, red. That makes us human. That makes us all the same, so these lessons really changed my life and really made me begin to appreciate who I am as an African and to appreciate and be proud of my heritage and to not apologise for it at all. It made me appreciate who I was as a black woman who would not conform to societal expectations by looking like someone she is not. I began to show openly more interest in my culture, my heritage. I began to look at not just women but people in general who live their lives unapologetically and learn all I could from them. It makes me be even more proud of who I am.

I know I am somebody that has overcome odds and I know that you can too. For women of colour, know that it's OK if right now you feel that the racism you experienced is not going to be something that you'll get over but the advice I would offer that helped me is to simply just BE YOU. In this modern time, I feel like almost everything is artificial. Don't be afraid to be your true self and don't compromise who you are for anything or anybody.

I stated all of the above to say again - I DID NOT FIT IN. I worked so hard trying to compare myself to everyone else and trying to make myself someone else that I lost who I was in the process. I became someone I didn't even recognise; didn't know any more and more importantly, didn't even like because this person was not real. This person was not me. This person was not who I saw when I looked in the mirror; it was somebody totally different. The real me was suffocating and I needed to get her back. I really believed people (especially the ones I loved) when they would tell me to be somebody else or something else and that I'd be better being something else.

I worked hard comparing myself to everyone else with everything I did. I would wear clothes that everyone was wearing just to fit in even though that style was not me. It was HARD to fit in. I would even eat foods that I really didn't like just so that I would be appreciated or at least feel appreciated and accepted. The situation was so bad - I became a whole other person. I would change my accent to talk like the people around me and really was uncomfortable with this because the real me in my accent would show up often and I'd feel so exposed as if my accent was something I should be ashamed of. It was so draining. All I did was focus on what I thought were the bad things or negative things about me and I didn't realise that I had so many good qualities, so much to bring to the table, that there was and is no one like me and there never will be.

No one has my unique gifts. There's only one Nana and that's alright. I have so much to contribute and offer and I am enough. This is what led me to deal with training for counselling and wanting to help women realise their true authentic selves and understand their true authentic voice; and not to be afraid to be who they are. Not everybody is going to agree with you. Not everybody is going to like you but guess what, not everybody was put on earth to agree with you and not everybody was put on earth to like you so be okay with that. That's not going to change.

So, what does being and living unapologetically look like? Firstly, I can't stress enough the importance about setting boundaries. When you are dealing with bullies, pushy and manipulative and narcissistic people who try to force you to be someone and something you are not, it can be scary to set boundaries with them but it's the most important step to take. Even if these people are members of your own family. They need to learn and understand how to treat you and accept what you will and will not tolerate and you should not feel guilty for setting these boundaries - your spiritual, mental, emotional, and even physical health depend on it.

One of my favourite writers, Paulina Xenia puts it this way, "being unapologetic is about validating yourself and being so accepting of yourself that you no longer need to seek outside validation or approval to feel good enough or worthy." I do a lot of volunteer work with counselling and one of the things I've learned from counselling women is that a lot of women feel the same way I do. They feel like they can't be who they really are and believe me when I tell you that all of them are so gifted and talented and are doing amazing things that they just needed to see that its ok to be different. Its ok to have a talent or gift that no one gets. That doesn't make you a bad person. It makes you unique and there is a void in life that only you can fill. No one else is like you at all. From your DNA to your character, you have a lot to offer the world so go out there and do it.

Secondly, don't get me wrong, being unapologetic does not mean you have to express your opinion all the time or shout it every time you face someone whose opinion is different from yours, but it does mean listening to the other person and not compromising on yours. That's why I'm so proud to write this story even if it's just to say you don't have to be ashamed of who you are; you're not alone. Even if you feel different, even if you feel unusual, even if you feel that no one else will understand you, you are unique. You are made unique and it's about time you realised that and it's about time you celebrated that and it's about time you understand that. I can be me and be unapologetic about it. That's what's so exciting about writing this. It is knowing that if I can encourage just one person to be authentically themselves then I've accomplished my goal. So, the theme of this story is *shine your light so bright*. Be who YOU are. There is nobody that can be you better than YOU and that's a good thing.

More about Nana

Nana is a British born Zambian who is very passionate about seeing women realise their full potential. A big supporter and believer in women supporting women. She is also a huge believer that people of the world from different backgrounds and races and nationalities can actually get along and contribute to society in a positive way.

Nana has worked with nonprofit organisations such as World Vision and the United Nations which is where she leaned into her passion for humanitarian work. Nana is currently based in the UK where she serves as co-director for the Joinher Network.

Meet Amanda Maynard-Schubert

It was in this dark moment that I heard it—my voice. The voice that had been buried and drowned out by years of false personas, of masks and false truths that I had convinced myself were real. The clarity of the path ahead was tangible, and it echoed through every fibre of my being.

https://www.facebook.com/amanda.schubert.771

https://www.linkedin.com/in/amanda-schubert-51b0671a8/

Lighting The Way

I spent a great deal of my life not liking who I was. I had no justifiable reason to feel this way—I am not even sure where the resentment first began. All I knew is the seed was planted and eventually grew to an all-encompassing belief, a fundamental part of my core. And it has taken me a long time to prune back the barbed thorns and free myself from the cage I had created. To feel content. To look at myself in the mirror and smile.

To be unapologetically me.

It's not so much that I had what may be called a 'bad' life (not that life can be so easily divided into good or bad—we work in shades of grey, not black and white). I had a loving family, great friends, a roof over my head and food on the table. But even the most apparently-perfect person with an ideal life can be plagued by doubt and wonder if they will ever be good enough. Self-worth doesn't discriminate between people; between the rich and poor, the young or old, or anyone, anywhere. No matter where you come from, or who you are, or the circumstances in which you find yourself, anyone can be hit with those moments of wondering who they are, or why they are here.

There has long been an underlying force that drives people, across the centuries and generations—what is our purpose? Some have devoted their entire lives to finding the answer to that question. Is it happiness? Is it love? Is it to serve others, or to live entirely for ourselves and leave no regrets behind when we go out in a blaze of glory? There as many answers are there are souls on the planet, and every answer is unique. So, what is it, then? What are we here for? What are we to do with our time on earth, to get to the end of our timeline and say to ourselves that we lived a 'good' life? If we haven't achieved everything we wanted to, does that mean we have failed? Is life really just one big test that we will never get the grade for?

For much of my younger years, this plagued me. This idea that my life was a race that I had to win, or else. When others were moving faster than me, or doing better than me, did it mean I was losing? Was I destined to chase everyone else for the rest of my life, never quite catching up and stumbling over the finish line with no achievements to my name other than existing? Those are some big questions to ponder for a child. Yet it forms so much of our early development. "What do you want to be when you grow up?" "Find a career that will set you up for life, then rise to the top of your field." "Make sure you save your money to buy a house and start a family."

That's a lot of pressure for young shoulders to carry. Heck, it's a lot of pressure for a thirty-something adult to carry. And I like to think I'm pretty strong!

I remember my time at school as being a mix of great joy, but also overwhelming stress, particularly once I reached high school. I was bullied often through my early years, though that tailed off a little at high school. The scars were still painful, though. Those deep wounds to my self-worth and sense of wellbeing cut to my core, to the very heart of who I believed I was, and who I could be. Bullying is still a severe issue occurring in schools today, and, unfortunately, there is no simple solution to fixing it. The impact it has on children cannot be underestimated, and it is an area that everyone should be concerned about and working toward healing in our communities.

For me, the full impact of those years of being teased and belittled wouldn't be felt until my late-teens, when I was preparing to launch myself into life as an adult. Around the middle of high school, the focus shifts from one of general education to targeted learning designed to propel us into our chosen careers. University, TAFE, apprenticeships—all become the centre of the students' universe. Gone is the time for fun and games; adulthood is beckoning, and you MUST have a plan for your life. Will you study at university? What course will you choose? Will you take a gap year, or dive straight into it? Have you considered the pros and cons of both? If not university, then surely you will study a trade at TAFE, or enter into an apprenticeship? You simply *cannot* leave here without a course of action. The whole idea is unthinkable. Oh, by the way, you also need to navigate relationships, come to terms with your changing body, and possibly work a job after hours if you hope to have money and get ahead.

'Get ahead'. This simple phrase sums up where the whole idea of life being a race stems from. By its very definition, it implies that, somehow, we are born into a competition. That from the moment we take our first breath out in the open air, we are already 'winning' or 'losing'. Then the rest of our life will be devoted to either staying ahead of the pack so that we come out on top, or fighting for every inch so that we don't get left behind. Because heaven help us if we reach the end of our lives in last place.

Now, this doesn't mean that we should not have ambitions, or hopes and dreams. Goals are important. Having something to strive for, something we believe in and want to see come to fruition provides great satisfaction and gives that sense of purpose that stirs our souls into action. But goals should be set by *us* for *ourselves*. When a goal has been given to us by someone else, or we think we must achieve certain targets in order to please others, then we are no longer living for our happiness. This was the trap I fell into, and one I took a long time to escape.

I found the quickest path for me to gain acceptance by my peers was to mould myself into what they wanted me to be. I was quiet when I needed to be, I learned to be quick-witted and sharp with my tongue, and I took on this persona of bravado and an attitude of not caring. By hiding my true self under a different mask for every person I met, I became a chameleon, and I stayed safe. Falling seamlessly into the crowd and no longer standing out. My true self was safely tucked away, and I could be who they wanted me to be. Surely this would lead to me finally being happy?

Drawing to the end of my high school years, I had no clear direction for my life. Having lost myself completely at that point,

I had no desire to pursue any goals, to aim for any targets. My dreams were non-existent. How can one dream when they have no identity anymore? So, I coasted through my senior year, choosing to stay in school to be with my friends rather than use that time to pursue a career or study toward getting into a tertiary course. My plan for my life? Be with my friends as much as possible. Maybe get a job to make some money, since that's kind of important. Other than that, I didn't care. I was never going to win this race, anyway, so why torture myself trying to 'get ahead'? What was the point?

For a few years, I job-hopped, not settling in any real place for more than a few months at a time. I'd start working somewhere, then realise I was miserable, so I'd move on to something else. Always looking for something better, but never finding it. With the wisdom of hindsight, I realise now that I was aimless and misdirected because I had shut myself off from my soul, from my essence. I could no longer hear my unique voice, the calling of my heart, and I was trying to find some way to get back to it. To rediscover what I had lost.

It was only when I met my future-husband that some glimmer of my true self sparked back into life. In him, I saw someone who reflected my own struggle. Someone who had been hurt and was still recovering from losing his own identity and sense of self. It was in this relationship that I first felt the stirrings of my soul's mission, though I would not realise this for quite some time yet. But there is much that I owe to this pivotal moment in time.

Not long after we got married, my husband and I produced two beautiful children. At the time of my first child's birth, I was working in the local hospital in the catering department. As much as I enjoyed my job, I now had a new focus for my time and energy, and I found returning to work very challenging. Back came the old niggles; how could I expect to save for a new house and set my family up with a 'good' life if I left work? How was I ever supposed to 'get ahead' without a stable income? Anxiety became a very prominent aspect of my life around this time, and although my heart was full of joy at becoming a mother, the constant struggle to maintain the persona that the world had come to expect of me while nourishing my soul calling almost became too much to bear.

It was in this dark moment that I heard it—my voice. The voice that had been buried and drowned out by years of false personas, of masks and false truths that I had convinced myself were real. The clarity of the path ahead was tangible, and it echoed through every fibre of my being. No matter what it took, I would be home with my daughter. The desire to be there for her, to put aside the jobs I had only ever done because I 'had to' and devote my time and energy to raising her, to teaching her and loving her with my whole heart, overrode any notion that I needed to continue to run the rat race with everybody else. Just like that, I got off the track and started down my own path.

Was it easy? Not at all. It required sacrifice, it meant budgeting and time management, and often putting aside wants for needs.

Of course, we were met with opposition and doubt, often from well-meaning people who couldn't understand why my husband and I would go without certain 'must-haves' to allow me to be a stay-at-home mother. In this day and age, status and success tend to be measured by possessions—the size of the home, the quality of the car, the televisions, the iPads, and the Thermomixes. How could we possibly hope to keep up with the status quo on one modest income?

Our answer was always simple: "We'll make it work." It became something of a mantra for our little family. No matter what came our way, we would work together to find a solution and turn the circumstances in our favour. At times, this was harder than expected, and we very nearly lost everything. But through sheer determination, and continuing to be guided by our gut feelings, we found ourselves able to purchase our first home a few years later, once my son was born.

Having someone like my husband, someone who supported me one hundred percent, who believed in me with his whole heart, made all the difference. When we find someone who truly sees us, someone who looks beyond the surface and connects with us on a soul level, then magic can truly happen. This doesn't always come in the form of a romantic partner—it could be a parent, a friend, a relative, or even someone we work with. And it is made all the more special when you find many of them; people who *see* you. The feeling is unlike any other. When you connect with those people, every fibre of your being seems to come alive, and there is a wonderful sense of wholeness and contentedness that melts through your entire existence.

My big epiphany moment came sometime later, after my children had both started school and I went searching for work once more. After spending so many glorious years devoting my time and attention to raising my family and creating a warm and loving home, it was now time to spread my wings and refocus the direction of my life. Moving through stages is pivotal to any sort of growth; we see it all the time in nature. Time is fluid, and all things flow along their path, constantly shifting and changing with the tides. Nothing in this universe stays stagnant, it is constantly in a state of flux. Humans are no exception. No matter how long or short our time on earth may be, we can never remain in one fixed state—and I could feel the tug of a new phase emerging in my very soul.

However, old patterns were unfolding as I tried to find work. I would start a job, be happy, then slowly start to develop anxiety and resentment in my workplaces, unable to commit myself to any particular role. At first, the old insecurities began to knock on my self-esteem, yelling at me that I was not good enough, that I was letting my family down, and that people would begin to think I was a terrible person because I was so unreliable. But something had shifted now. The venomous whispers of that voice didn't seem to carry the same crippling weight. It was suddenly easier to block it out, to brush off the snide remarks and keep carrying on.

Why? Because I was finally beginning to feel worthy. I could look back over how far I had come, and appreciate the journey for what it was. As vital as it had been for me to feel seen by others, I could now see myself with fresh eyes. Thanks to the connections I had made, for the people who had given me the space and freedom to let my guard down, to remove the masks I had maintained for so long, my true self was beginning to blossom. And I realised that I was actually happy with who I was.

This was revolutionary.

So much of my life had been spent trying to please others, to make them like me by becoming who they needed me to be. The weight of other people's opinions had buried me for so long that I no longer realised quite how heavy that burden had become. When it lifted, it was almost overwhelming. The sheer freedom that came from discarding all of my shields and disguises left me feeling rather vulnerable and exposed. It was scary and exhilarating all at the same time.

Like a snake shedding its skin, the layers of doubt and false identity that I had been living through began to fall away. At times this was painful, and many relationships that I had believed to have been built on mutual respect and love crumbled and faded away. As my soul began to awaken, the aspects of my life that were no longer serving me were highlighted and removed, clearing the way for the new opportunities and people to come into my life. My new phase was beginning.

One aspect of myself that had lain in wait, neglected and discarded, was my spiritual side. Growing up in a deeply religious community, this was one of the first things that I shoved deep down inside, lest people should label me as a 'hippie', or 'woo-woo'. But my desire to rediscover this part of myself had been activated and would no longer be silenced. I learned to read Tarot cards, I collected crystals and essential oils, and began secretly offering readings to people through cards and channelled messages. I deepened my connection with nature, spending more time out with the trees and the water, allowing myself the freedom to explore and learn. I studied Wicca and Buddhism and received my attunement to Reiki healing. All the things I had denied myself for so long, things I had been too scared to try in case people thought less of me, or thought I was different. That I didn't belong.

I had always been a strong empath, though I didn't always understand it. I had been able to read people's emotions and motivations for a very long time and had used this to aid me in choosing the right persona to adopt in my interactions with them. But now, I turned this skill into something far more beneficial. I began to see people. To truly *see* them. Rather than using this ability as self-defence, as a means to avoid making the wrong move and causing someone to dislike me, I was now allowing my own shields to come down so that I could help others. It was quite a radical shift for me.

See, I was no longer hiding myself out of fear. While I still kept quite a few aspects of myself hidden, this was now a conscious choice, and one that I had control over. The motivation behind it now came from a place of self-confidence and assurance, not one of anxiety and a desire to please others. In the past, I had felt as though I were trapped in a tornado, being constantly thrown and yanked about against my will, my own voice lost in the wild rush of external forces. But here, now, I was centred and calm, in a place of quiet acceptance as the world moved around me.

This perspective carries so much strength. When we find our centre, we are no longer driven by the circumstances around us, feeling out of control or like everything is too overwhelming. In this space, no matter what is happening around you, there is a sense of peace, of security that you can handle whatever comes your way. This is the true strength that is found in authenticity, of owning your power. It does not come from others, from what someone believes you are, or what circumstances you are in. This place resides inside you, and is always there, no matter what is happening around you.

With this new-found strength, I began to live life on my terms. My desire to please others had originally come from good intentions; I love caring for others and nurturing them, but I had misinterpreted this feeling as a need to make them like me. Now, instead of bending over backwards to serve others at my own expense, I found myself drawn to aiding them to bring out their best. No longer did I feel bound by the need to change myself to make them happy. Rather, I wanted to show them how to see themselves the way I saw them; to spread kindness and compassion because that is who I am, and not because someone expects it of me.

Eventually, following my intuition and trusting in myself led me to making one of the most important decisions of my life. An opportunity presented itself to travel to Ireland on a writer's retreat. Ireland had always been a place I had longed to visit, and a place I felt connected to on a far deeper than just somewhere to go. So, that had already made me determined to go, but the fact that it would also provide me with an opportunity to work with and learn from established authors and publishers. The dream of one day writing a book and becoming an author was one that I had abandoned during my school years, convinced that it was not something I would ever be able to achieve. But here, right in front of me, was the chance to breathe life back into that part of me. And I was not going to miss out.

With the help of my family, I saved up the money I needed to get there and started putting a draft of my potential novel together, ready to take with me. I was giddy with excitement at the possibilities ahead of me, and the burgeoning reality that I may achieve my goal of publishing a novel. Then, a month before I was due to fly out, I was struck with the most intense episode of self-doubt that I had had in years. I was an absolute wreck, and was convinced that I was making a huge mistake; my story was terrible, I was selfish for leaving my family behind while I travelled to the other side of the world, and I was wasting too much of our hard-earned money. What was I thinking?

However, when the day came to board my flight, that is exactly what I did. Despite the doubt, despite the nerves, and despite the wave of unworthiness that had threatened to overwhelm me, I was on my way to Ireland. I was backing myself and going after my dream with everything I had, and the feeling of empowerment that fired through my soul in that moment was pure magic. I arrived at the writer's retreat ready to absorb and make the most of every single opportunity that came my way, because this was my moment. This was the moment my path forwards lit up before me and I knew what it was I wanted to do.

As part of our retreat, all the attending authors were invited to speak to a room of invited guests, consisting of high school students, local Irish authors, and other special guests. As much as the idea of speaking to a crowd terrified me (I had never enjoyed public speaking, having once thrown up in front of my entire class at school when giving a presentation), I saw this opportunity for what it was; a chance to acknowledge the journey I had taken to be there and inspire others who, perhaps like me, were struggling to find their way. This idea warmed my heart, and I found myself relaxing completely into the moment, and presenting my talk with all the passion and joy that I could muster. This talk was not *about* me, not really—it was for anyone in the room that day who needed to hear the words their soul recognised but could not say out loud. For those who needed to feel seen, as I had needed to be. And I was honoured to be given the space to share that.

Since then, I have published two award-winning novels, contributed to four anthologies, with several more in the works, and have settled well and truly into the life of an author. I wake up each day with the knowledge that I am doing something I love, and it fuels my soul like no other career has. But it is not just about the books. What has truly ignited me and given me a new zest and sense of purpose is connecting with people. More specifically, young people—those on the cusp of discovering who they are and who they have the potential to be.

Even before my first book was published, I have always wanted to write in the Young Adult genre. I remember being that age, from around ten years old, and feeling so out-of-touch with my peers and my place in the world. My greatest source of comfort and inspiration then was books. Tamora Pierce has, and probably will always be, my greatest influence as an author, as it was her series of books that got me through those toughest times, inspiring me with her tales of strong, independent female characters who were achieving incredible things while still remaining completely relatable. Her characters experienced doubt, they made mistakes and learned from them, and they went through all the awkward phases of being a teen, then a young adult. Raw, genuine and inspiring.

I knew that this was what I wanted to evoke with my own books and stories—characters that young people could see themselves in, who could show them that they are not alone in their struggles and uncertainties, and who may not be perfect, but they keep trying to be the best they can be. In this day and age, building connections with people is sometimes more difficult than it has been in previous generations. With the rise of digital communication, we are more available to people, yet much of our interaction now is shallow and achieved via email, text or through video calls. The true impact of the current Covid crisis will also not be known for some time, particularly for those children who have grown up during the years of isolation, social distancing, and limited physical contact, such as hugs and other shows of affection. The need for connection is more vitally important than ever.

Through my role as an author, an important, yet unexpected, path has opened up for me; one that I believe may actually have been where my soul was trying to guide me in the first place. As part of my work, I spend a lot of time visiting schools and talking to young people about my work and how I became an author. I also get recognised down the street far more often, when people stop me to tell me that they've read my work, or to offer kind words of encouragement or admiration for what I have achieved. Looking back at how often I worried that I was not good enough, or thinking that people may not like me, it is a strange sort of feeling. Even more so is knowing that I am inspiring others. I never believed this would be how people would see me. I now know, though, that this was because I didn't see myself. Not truly.

Now, I know the importance of allowing my light to shine. When I used to hide myself away, I thought I was protecting myself from the opinions of others, and that is what I needed to do to fit in, to be accepted. But now I know that the greatest thing I can do is to truly live life on my terms and allow myself to be authentic in every way. By living unapologetically, by owning my power and honouring my path, I not only free myself, but I also free others of the weight of responsibility for my self-worth. Because it is not up to them to provide me with courage, or joy, or acceptance. It is not their job to make me feel like I am worthy, or special, or that what I do matters. The power lies solely with me, and me alone. Only when I acknowledge this can I truly honour my soul and live my life with meaning and purpose.

Sharing this knowledge with children and young adults is where my path has taken me. I am finding myself drawn specifically to the kids who feel like they don't matter, who have or are going through the same struggles that I did, and who cannot see their worth because so much of their identity is impacted by the actions and words of others.

By giving these kids a voice, by seeing them when they feel like they are invisible, I hope to leave a lasting legacy that empowers the next generation to believe in themselves and what they are capable of. To take away the pressure and the stigma that life is a competition that only the lucky or the privileged can ever hope to win. You are not defined by your home, your job, your IQ, or how much money you have in the bank. Making yourself miserable by constantly striving to achieve the dreams and expectations of others will not benefit anyone in the long run. One of my favourite quotes, and one that I am constantly inspired by, is by the late Rita Pierson: "Every child deserves a champion. An adult who will never give up on them, who understands the power of connection, and insists that they become the best that they can possibly be."

I don't shrink myself down anymore. I wear my scars proudly and through my words and my actions, I live authentically and honour my ever-evolving journey. When I make a mistake, or don't act with integrity or truth, I don't belittle myself or believe that I am unworthy or a failure. Instead, I acknowledge that I am human, and that living means navigating both the high mountains and the low valleys along the way. It is through being my true self that I can light the way for others, and I no longer feel the need to try to impress people or change who I am to fit their expectations. I spent so much of my life hiding and dulling my spark, but I now see myself in the light. I see my soul, I see my power, and I see the path laid out for me.

And I have never loved myself more.

More about Amanda

Born and raised in the Riverland region of South Australia, Amanda is an author with a passion for all things fantasy. An avid reader as a child, it was Amanda's dream to one day write and publish her own series of books. Inspired by authors like Tamora Pierce and J.R.R. Tolkien, Amanda's writing weaves magic, mythology and elemental mysteries to create enchanting worlds and stories. Her debut novel, 'The Bards of Birchtree Hall', was released in November 2020. The first book in 'The Stormbringer Chronicles', it earned a 5-star review from Reader's Favorite and was awarded the international Literary Titan Gold Award for excellence. The second book in the series, 'The Vengeance of the Morrígan', was released in November 2021.

Under the pen name 'Mandy May', Amanda's work has featured in 'Sweet Delights', a romance anthology by Gumnut Press, and under the name 'Amanda Schubert', she has been published in the inspirational anthology, 'The Colours of Me', by Making Magic Happen Press. In 2021, she was a finalist in the Roar Success Awards in the category of 'Best Author/Writer/Blogger'. Her book, 'The Bards of Birchtree Hall', was also gifted to the 2021 Oscar nominees as part of the Hollywood Swag Bag Honouring Oscar Nominees Weekend gift bags.

When not busy writing, Amanda enjoys spending time in the garden with her husband and two children, enjoying the magic of nature and the elements.

CPSIA information can be obtained
at www.ICGtesting.com
Printed in the USA
LVHW071650150222
711211LV00020B/654